Winston Churchill
The Greatest Briton

WINSTON CHURCHILL
The Greatest Briton

DOMINIQUE ENRIGHT

MICHAEL O'MARA BOOKS LIMITED

First published in Great Britain in 2003 by
Michael O'Mara Books Limited
9 Lion Yard, Tremadoc Road
London SW4 7NQ

A CIP catalogue record for this book
is available from the British Library

Extracts from the works of Winston S. Churchill
are reproduced with permission of Curtis Brown Ltd,
London, on behalf of Winston S. Churchill.
Copyright Winston S. Churchill.

PHOTOGRAPH CREDITS:
TopFoto: pp. 13, 55, 89, 133, 157, 181;
Mary Evans Picture Library: pp. 29, 71, 111;
The Illustrated London News: pp. 167, 203, 221, 235.

ISBN 1-84317-049-3

1 3 5 7 9 10 8 6 4 2

Designed and typeset by Martin Bristow

Printed and bound in England
by Clays Ltd, St Ives plc

Contents

Introduction

'Energy and Poetry'

O NE DAY IN 1953, five-year-old Nicholas Soames, son of Churchill's daughter Mary Soames, was on a visit to Chartwell. The grown-ups were talking about Winston Churchill. He understood just one thing of what they were saying and hastened out of the room to have it confirmed by the horse's mouth. He ran upstairs. 'Grandpapa!' he cried, bursting into the big bedroom, where the Prime Minister was in bed working on a speech. 'Grandpapa, are you really the greatest man in the world?'

'Of course I am the greatest man in the world,' growled Churchill. *'Now bug— . . . buzz off.'*

'The characteristic of a great man is his power to leave a lasting impression on people he meets.'

By this criterion of greatness, his own, Winston Churchill must surely be accounted a great man, a judgement he would probably not have disagreed with, given the size of his ego, and his need for a loving audience. (*'I am not usually accused even by my friends of a modest or retiring disposition,'* he once remarked.) That

Churchill should, nearly forty years after his death, be voted the 'greatest Briton' might have surprised him, though – indeed it would probably have surprised him that such a vote should be taken at all – for as the author of a book on 'great contemporaries' he would have been all too aware of the difficulties inherent in making judgements of this type, and how, so often, circumstances have a part to play – in his case, the Second World War.

That he was a great man is indisputable – he was, indeed, larger than life in many respects. It can only be considered a blessing that he came first in a list of the top ten Britons, given the curious order in which the other 'candidates' came (not to mention the fact that some of them could not truly be termed 'great', famous as they might have been). He would have been very proud – possibly slightly overawed – to have come before Shakespeare, Nelson, Newton or Darwin. Where he had the advantage over these 'great Britons' was in his greater breadth of vision (partly, admittedly, owing to technological advantage), much of which was thanks to all his reading, and to his outstanding memory.

Most important of all, however, is that if it had not been for the bulldog tenacity with which he clung to his belief that Hitler posed a sinister and very serious danger to Europe, or for the strength of personality with which he carried everyone with him in the fight against Nazism, and his foresight in securing the United States and, later, the Soviet Union as allies, the world would today be very different – even, perhaps, in a kind of *dark age*, as he predicted to Britain.

It is not his achievements alone that made him great. There was something about his character that set him above normal people. It was not by any means a saintly character; he could in fact be utterly exasperating and was often needlessly rude. But there was warmth in him – he wanted people to be happy (and pleased with him); he could be spiteful and childishly petulant, but that made him more accessible. He was attractively child*like*, too; until the last years he took an interest in what was going on around him, and he made an effort to understand even complicated scientific topics. He also had vision, and was able to look forward and recognize how, for instance, the hydrogen bomb was that much more destructive than its predecessor, the atomic bomb. He was also incredibly courageous, and quite prepared to go out (with a certain swashbuckling air) into the worst of the fray.

A leading journalist wrote of him in 1908, long before he became well-known:

> He is extraordinarily youthful even for his years. He has the curiosity and animation of a child – a child in fairyland, a child consumed with the thirst for life. He must know all, taste all, devour all. He is drunk with the wonder and fascination of living. A talk with him is as exhilarating as a gallop across country, so full is it of adventure, and of the high spirits and eagerness of youth. No matter what the subject, soldiering or science, religion or literature, he plunges into it with the joy of a boy taking a 'header' in the sea. And to the insatiable curiosity and the enthusiasm of the boy he joins the frankness of the child. He has no reserves and no shams.

A very early biography, published in 1905, went rather over the top: 'In every work to which he has put his hand he has excelled. He will ever be a leader, whether of a forlorn hope or of a great party. Already in the House of Commons he leads by a natural right which no man can dispute.'

The enthusiasm of these two writers must in part be due to the effect Churchill himself had on them – he was able to make people feel good. Air Marshal Sir Arthur 'Bomber' Harris – a tough, unsentimental character – remarked that after visiting the Prime Minister he always felt 'invigorated and full of renewed hope and enthusiasm . . . I think the first thing that impresses one about Winston is the extraordinary mixture in him of real human kindness and of sometimes impish mischief, all overlaid with an immense, thrusting, purposeful determination to reach the goal which he so clearly sees.'

It is this 'feelgood' factor that came into play during the war. He made people, soldiers and those at home, genuinely believe that they could put up with deprivation, pain and suffering; that they would come through smiling; that they would defeat the enemy. He talked them into being strong and victorious.

'The first time you meet Winston you see all his faults, and the rest of your life you spend in discovering his virtues,' Pamela Plowden, an old flame of his who remained a lifelong friend, told a nervous, young just-appointed Private Secretary. And Field Marshal Sir Henry Wilson said much the same: 'He has many good qualities, some of which lie hidden, and he has many bad qualities, all of which are in the shop window.' Many of his employees started work for him prepared to dislike him – and soon became devoted to him. Selfish, malicious, demanding as he often was, he was also warm and kind. And he had the courage of his convictions. If his convictions turned out to be wrong, he was not afraid to change his mind.

President Roosevelt said to Churchill's personal detective, Inspector W. H. Thompson, as they were taking their leave after a meeting in August 1941: 'Look after the Prime Minister. He is one of the greatest men in the world.'

The tribute Clement Attlee – who had no reason to like Churchill, but clearly did – wrote in 1965 (in *Churchill: By His Contemporaries*, published by the *Observer*) would be difficult to better:

> By any reckoning, Winston Churchill was one of the greatest men that history records. If there were to be a gallery of great Englishmen that could accommodate only a dozen, I would like to see him in. He was brave, gifted, inexhaustible and indomitable . . .
>
> Energy, rather than wisdom, practical judgement or vision, was his supreme qualification . . . However, it is not the full story of what he did to win the war. It was the poetry of Churchill, as well, that did the trick. Energy and poetry, in my view, really sums him up.
>
> He was, of course, above all a supremely fortunate mortal . . . And perhaps the most warming thing about him was that he never ceased to say so.

DOMINIQUE ENRIGHT
August 2003

Chapter 1

Some Are Born Great

To Winston Churchill it was a matter of some pride that he just might have had a tiny bit of Iroquois blood in him: it was said that his American grandmother, Clara Hall, who married a New York businessman, Leonard Jerome, was one-eighth (or one-sixteenth, there is some dispute over that) Iroquois. Genealogical records show no evidence that Clara Hall's forebears included a native American – but it might be that it was kept from the church registers; while Clara Jerome's own alleged claim to being part Iroquois in an age when it would not have been readily admitted to does lend some credence to the story. Whatever the truth, Churchill himself believed he was part *'Red Indian'*. During the Second World War, he was sometimes the guest of President Franklin D. Roosevelt in New York; when Roosevelt told Churchill, with some pride, that his Dutch ancestors were among the very first settlers there, Churchill, it is said, was quick to retort, *'And it was my ancestors who greeted them.'*

Leonard Jerome, Churchill's grandfather, was something of a financial adventurer, familiar with the highs and lows of business and best known in the field of horse racing, as well as for his dalliances. When, following a whirlwind courtship, his daughter Jennie married Lord Randolph Churchill, a son of the seventh Duke of Marlborough, he was rather happier with the liaison than was the Duke. (That he was descended from the great military commander John Churchill, first Duke of Marlborough, was another source of pride to Winston Churchill.) A happy mix of social and military elite with New World commercial glamour and a rumoured touch of the exotic seems suitably unusual and alluring for someone who was to be hailed the 'greatest Briton'.

Lord and Lady Randolph's first child, Winston, was born prematurely on 30 November 1874 (*'Although present on the occasion, I have no clear recollection of the events leading up to it,'* he is reported to have commented) at Blenheim Palace, Oxfordshire, and was soon placed in the loving care of Mrs Everest, who became the boy's closest and most devoted confidante. As a baby, he must have resembled himself in old age: *'Madam, all babies look like me,'* he said, in his later years, to a woman who told him proudly that her baby looked like him. As a baby, too, he probably started to show his strength of character. Shortly after they moved to Dublin at the beginning of 1877, his mother wrote home, 'Winston is flourishing tho rather X the last 2 days more teeth I think.' He was two years old, which suggests that it was more likely to be normal toddler behaviour (i.e. temper tantrums), but writ large – as most aspects of Churchill were – than teeth.

The young Winston saw comparatively little of his parents. His father was a remote figure, and his mother scarcely less so. She was like *'a fairy princess: a radiant being possessed of limitless riches and power,'* he wrote in *My Early Life*. *'She shone for me like the Evening Star. I loved her dearly – but at a distance.'*

Shortly before his eighth birthday, Winston was sent to board at St George's School in Ascot, a school that even by Victorian standards was brutally disciplinarian. This did not suit a child used to the warmth of Mrs Everest and the detached affection of his parents, and perhaps helped to strengthen an already very wilful and defiant nature. While he might have responded to his beloved nanny's loving rebukes (though bribery tended to be more successful), the punishments meted out at his school probably served only to increase his rebelliousness.

What did not interest him, young Winston paid scant attention to. His favourite subjects – such as history and geography – he did very well in. Arithmetic he did not care for as it required careful working out, and you could only be right or wrong, not almost right – neither did having an excellent memory help. Latin and Greek he could see little point in as they were no longer spoken, and his first encounter with Latin was famously not a success: told to learn a declension – of *mensa* (table) – he did so without understanding it. Then, puzzled, he asked what the vocative was, to be told that 'You would use it in speaking to a table'. When he gave the reasonable if impudent response that he never did speak to tables, his teacher was far from amused and assured him that impertinence was punished severely.

'Composition: very feeble,' said his report for summer 1883: this for the boy who was to be awarded the Nobel Prize for Literature in 1953 – admittedly seventy years later, but his first book to be published (a history of the

Malakand Field Force) came out in 1898, barely fifteen years later, and over the years many more books followed. (In fact, he published in total more words than Charles Dickens and Walter Scott together – *'more books than Moses,'* he joked early enough in his career as author.) As for his spelling, said the report, it was 'about as bad as it well can be'. This has led to claims that he was dyslexic, but it was more likely to be because he was, as he himself later wrote, *'not lazy and untidy but careless and forgetful'*. Indeed, Churchill's feeling for the English language, and his ability with it, was quite extraordinary and certainly contributed to his greatness. 'He mobilized the English language and sent it into battle,' John F. Kennedy said in 1963, borrowing the words from the US's leading wartime radio reporter, Edward R. Murrow, in his 1940 introduction to his Churchill war speech excerpts. ('Now the hour had come for him to mobilize the English language, and send it into battle, a spearhead of hope for Britain and the world . . .')

Winston's French was deemed 'fair' by his masters at St George's. He seems to have enjoyed the subject: he later wrote of his next school, in Brighton, that *'I was allowed to learn things which interested me: French, History, and lots of Poetry by heart, and above all Riding and Swimming.'* He had a very slight speech defect, which made his 'Ss' sound like 'shs': this he turned to good effect in speaking his own language (and sometimes probably exaggerated if he felt that doing so would serve his ends, or at least afford him some amusement). It might well, however, have made him less confident in speaking foreign languages (although lack of confidence is not a feature associated with Churchill), or perhaps his impatient ego prevented him from working at the accent

– besides, it could be useful to pretend that one is not as fluent in a language as one actually is, even if only to inspire surprise and amusement, both valuable weapons.

'Be on your guard!' warned Churchill in a speech in Paris, shortly after the Liberation of France. *'I'm going to speak in French – a formidable undertaking and one which will put great demands upon your friendship for Great Britain.'* The French, proud as they are of their language, would probably have forgiven him any distortion of it at that moment – but such words would in any case have warmed them to him. (Georges Clemenceau's words uttered during the previous war held true now more than ever: 'Monsieur Churchill est loin d'être un ennemi de la France.' Churchill was indeed far from being an enemy of France.)

On another occasion when he was due to broadcast to the French in French, he rather offended the BBC's French expert, Monsieur Duchesne, when, having been settled in front of the microphone in the studio, he looked around and demanded, *'Where's my frog speech?'*. And he once startled a Free French general by explaining the Women's Voluntary Services as *'Les femmes qu'on ne paie pas'*.

He even ventured on verse in French, published in his book *Painting as a Pastime* (1948):

> *La peinture à l'huile*
> *Est bien difficile,*
> *Mais c'est beaucoup plus beau*
> *Que la peinture à l'eau.*

A couple of French officers must have dined out many times on the occasion when, at the Château du

Muguet in June 1940, for a meeting of the Supreme Council, they were sitting quietly drinking coffee in the dining room, when the doors flew open and, as reported by General Edward (known as Louis) Spears, 'an apparition which they said resembled an angry Japanese genie, in long, flowing, red silk kimono over other similar but white garments, girdled with a white belt' burst in, 'sparse hair on end', and loudly demanded, '*Oo ay ma ban?*' A creature of habit in matters concerning his daily domestic routine, he had assumed that somewhere in the château there was a bathtub full of steaming water waiting for him.

Clearly he had taken seriously a comment by his cousin, Charles Churchill, 9th Duke of Marlborough, in a letter of December 1912: 'I have been shocked at the manner in which you display your person when travelling to and from the bathroom, and I am making an effort to find you an appropriate leaf.' The 'appropriate leaf' was a dressing gown Marlborough had bought as a Christmas present for his cousin.

Another dressing-gown story comes from Detective-Inspector W. H. Thompson, who acted as bodyguard to Churchill for over nine years. This one reflects Churchill's sense of probity, rather than his bathtime habits. In the mid-1920s, when Churchill was Chancellor of the Exchequer, he implemented import duties on artificial fabrics in order to protect Britain's rayon manufacturers. As a token of gratitude he was presented with two very fine rayon dressing gowns, one for himself and one for his wife; but he would not accept them as a gift, insisting on writing out a cheque for them, which was then handed on to a charity.

*

Run-ins with de Gaulle were not uncommon, and the Frenchman probably had a fair idea of Churchill's level of French, but, during negotiations at Casablanca in 1943, where he was trying to reconcile Generals de Gaulle and Giraud, Churchill startled de Gaulle by snapping sharply at him: '*Si vous m'obstaclerez, je vous liquiderai.*'

As Churchill's Private Secretary in 1941, John ('Jock') Colville was on one occasion caught uncomfortably between the two statesmen. General de Gaulle was at the time 'obstaclering' Churchill, who, annoyed, summoned him to Downing Street. Beforehand he informed Colville that he would not shake hands with de Gaulle and would not speak with him in French but through an interpreter – and that Colville himself was to be the interpreter.

The General arrived at the due time and was ushered into the Cabinet Room. True to his word, Churchill did not shake his hand, merely indicating a seat across the table from himself. '*General de Gaulle, I have asked you to come here this afternoon,*' he started and looked fiercely at Colville, who translated: 'Mon Général, je vous ai invité . . .'

'*I* didn't *say "Mon Général",*' Churchill broke in, '*and I did not say I had* invited *him.*'

This continued for a few more sentences, Churchill interrupting continually with objections to Colville's translation. Then de Gaulle spoke and Colville interpreted – to be interrupted by '*Non, non. Ce n'est pas du tout le sens de ce que je disais.*' Colville was pretty certain that he had understood de Gaulle's meaning, and had conveyed it correctly – but Churchill said that if Colville could not do any better he had better find someone who could. A half-ashamed, half-relieved Colville escaped and urgently summoned an official from the Foreign Office whose French was impeccable. The gentleman arrived in next to no time and Colville showed him into the Cabinet Room (in which not a word had been spoken during the interval).

Within minutes the man from the Foreign Office erupted from the Cabinet Room, red-faced, and spluttering that they had to be mad: they had said he could not speak French properly and they would have to manage without an interpreter.

The soundproof double doors of the Cabinet Room were closed and nothing could be heard. Over an hour passed and Colville was beginning to get anxious – 'Perhaps they had strangled each other?' But eventually the bell rang and he went in to find the two men sitting amicably side by side, smoking cigars and chatting – in French.

It is clear that while he might have enjoyed French as a subject at school, Churchill felt that in his dealings with foreigners in their language it should be always on his terms. Just as he knew the power of his own language to move people, so did he recognize that his massacring of foreign tongues could be a useful weapon – he knew, for instance, that, petty as it was, the irritation caused to the Nazi Party by his calling them '*Narzees*' weakened their position, if very slightly. And if anyone should object – why, '*Everybody has a right to pronounce foreign names as he chooses.*' A friend of his, Jack Seely (Lord Mottistone) recalled Churchill explaining to him: '*Jack, when* you *cross Europe you land at Marsai, spend a night in Lee-on and another in Par-ee, and, crossing by Callay, eventually reach Londres. I land at Mar-sales, spend a night in Lions, and another in Paris, and come home to London.'*

In a world leader, such childish behaviour, however unacceptable, had to be accepted, exasperating as it could be, but at his first school, conduct of this sort was not tolerated and was generally rewarded with a flogging. His diligence seems to have left something to be desired, too: the report quoted earlier also complained that 'He does not understand the meaning of hard work', while another report maintained: 'He is a constant trouble to everybody and is always in some scrape or other. He cannot be trusted to behave himself anywhere.' In the years to come many co-members in the House of Commons would have heartily agreed with the last statement, as would a number of world leaders.

Many years later, Churchill's granddaughter, Celia Sandys, found, at St George's School, a written account by a fellow pupil, Harry Graf Kessler, who remembered Churchill as

a red-haired and restless boy, rather small for his age, who through his exhibitionism and quarrelsome attitude got on everyone's nerves. As a result of the time he had spent in the stables at Blenheim, Winston had learned words which were highly unsuitable for a young man. Mr Kynnersley, the headmaster, reacted with shock and apprehension against the not unlikely possibility that the entire school might adopt the spicy expressions of stable lads. When Winston, who was quite tiny – he was only just eight years old – leapt around a classroom table and recited to an attentive group of boys a little song from the stables, Mr Kynnersley threatened the use of the birch.

'*How I hated this school,*' Churchill wrote later. He was not there for very long, however: his health was not good, not helped by the floggings, and when he fell ill, his parents transferred him to a school in healthy seaside Brighton, where their family doctor was now practising. At this school he found '*an element of kindness and of sympathy*', and the three years he spent there left '*a pleasant picture*' in his mind.

This was the school where he was allowed to concentrate on the subjects that interested him. It cannot be said that he shone academically, but he did do better; or that his behaviour improved vastly – indeed for conduct he was usually bottom of the class. In an early report, his headmistress wrote that there had been 'a decided improvement in attention to work towards the latter part of the term', adding the gentle but pointed reproof that the marks 'are almost valueless as frequent absence from the schoolroom made competition with other boys very difficult'. (He could not always be blamed for absence from the schoolroom, however: while he was at this school he fell seriously ill with pneumonia – and sufficiently gravely for his parents to hurry to the school from London. In many affectionate letters from his schools the young Winston had begged them to visit him – but they had always been too busy.)

Lateness was a prevailing problem at school, and it remained so through Churchill's life. Indeed, it has been remarked that the only time he arrived early was in his premature birth. After that came a string of complaints about his lateness – 'Total times late – 19,' wrote the headmaster of St George's (this was over a period of about six weeks). While his house master at Harrow said in a letter to Lady Randolph, 'I do not think . . . that he is in any way wilfully troublesome: but his forgetfulness, carelessness, unpunctuality, and irregularity in every way, have really been so serious, that I write to ask you, when he is at home to speak very gravely to him on the subject.'

In later years, Churchill conceded that he was unpunctual – recollecting the occasion when, as a young second lieutenant in 1896 he was invited, as was his commanding officer, to a weekend party for the Prince of Wales (later Edward VII) for which *'I realized that I must be on my best behaviour – punctual, subdued, reserved – in short, display all the qualities with which I am least endowed.'* He arrived late to be met with a severe 'Don't they teach you to be punctual in your regiment, Winston?' from the Prince. Nevertheless, in *My Early Life*, there is a certain indulgent tone in his pronouncement: *'I do think unpunctuality is a vile habit, and all my life I have tried to break myself of it.'* And there is more than an element of the self-congratulatory in his assertion, *'I am a sporting man. I always like to give trains and aeroplanes a fair chance of getting away.'*

He certainly did not seem to suffer from 'train fever': in the early spring of 1899, Churchill left India, where he'd been fighting on the North-West Frontier, for Egypt. A young American girl on board the ship, Christine Lewis, with whom he made friends, recalled his late arrival: 'The gangplank was about to be raised when down the wharf ran a freckled, red-haired young man in a rumpled suit carrying an immense tin cake box. Although he had nearly missed the boat, he seemed utterly unruffled and, seating himself by the rail because there was not another spot left on deck, he carefully examined the other passengers.'

Eddie Marsh, who was Churchill's Private Secretary for most of the years between 1905 and 1929, summed up his child-like attitude to time perfectly: 'Winston's disregard of time, when there's anything he wants to do, is sublime – he firmly believes that it waits for him.'

As he neared the end of his time at the Misses Thompson's establishment, the young Winston, now twelve years old, *'entered the inhospitable regions of examinations'.* Many will sympathize with his view as expounded in *My Early Life*: *'The subjects which were dearest to the examiners were almost invariably those I fancied least. I would have liked to have been examined in history, poetry and writing essays. The examiners, on the other hand, were partial to Latin and mathematics . . . Moreover, the questions which they asked on both these subjects were almost invariably those to which I was unable to suggest a satisfactory answer. I should have liked to be asked to say what I knew. They always tried to ask what I did not know . . . This sort of treatment had only one result: I did not do well in examinations.'* (In fact, in saying that the examiners always asked him what he did not know, he was wrong – the day before taking an early Army exam, at Harrow, which involved drawing a map from memory, he picked on New Zealand to revise purely by chance. New Zealand it was in the exam, and Winston triumphed.)

These first exams were in order to enter Harrow, a good move in the view of his astute grandmother, the Duchess of Marlborough, 'for I fancy he was too clever and too much the Boss at that Brighton school'. (She seems to have felt obliged to tell Lord and Lady Randolph what their older son was like, writing to them some years later, in 1894: 'he is affectionate and pleasant, but you know he is mercurial' . . . and that she was the person to keep him in order, for 'you know he requires checking sometimes'.)

In *My Early Life*, Churchill describes amusingly how he spent two hours not answering the Latin paper, and tells us that on the strength of this – or, rather, on the strength of the other papers, which he does not mention – he was admitted into Harrow. His next few years did not glitter academically ('your work is an insult to your intelligence,' his mother on one occasion wrote crossly); but he clearly showed signs of brilliance – especially in his English and history essays, even though he did not always write the ones he'd been asked to write – that were noted by his teachers. He also won a prize for reciting twelve hundred lines of Macaulay's *Lays of Ancient Rome*, and for a poem entitled 'Influenza'. He was far from being the '*dunce*' he liked to pretend he was.

Nevertheless, it took him '*three tries*' to scrape into the Royal Military College, Sandhurst. After he left Harrow, Churchill's parents sent him to a '*crammer*' run by a Captain James, who doubtless found him one of his more interesting but also more trying pupils: 'I think the boy means well but he is distinctly inclined to be inattentive and to think too much of his abilities . . . he has been rather too much inclined up to the present to teach his instructors instead of endeavouring to learn from them.' In spite of a three-month absence from the crammer (arising from one of Churchill's more foolhardy escapades, a failed jump from a bridge to a tree during a game, which left him badly concussed and with a ruptured kidney), Captain James eventually succeeded with him.

Lord Randolph was disappointed that his son had not done well enough for the infantry – 'for in that failure you demonstrated beyond refutation your slovenly happy-go-lucky harum-scarum style of work for which you have always been distinguished at your different schools.' He was, however, to live just long enough to see his son pass out of the college, in December 1894, with flying colours, eighth out of 150 candidates. (Churchill's conduct at Sandhurst was, incidentally, classed 'good but unpunctual'.)

This then, the future 'greatest Briton' – a wilful, rebellious, impulsive, affectionate boy, careless, impatient of anything that didn't take his immediate fancy, fond of having his own way, only diligent where his interest was captured, tiresome, never on time, usually inattentive and inclined to answer back. If he'd been her child, his granddaughter Celia Sandys remarked, she would have adored him – but 'he wasn't the sort of child you'd want to stay for the holidays'.

Chapter 2
Some Achieve Greatness

IN THE YEARS THAT FOLLOWED, achievement seemed to be Churchill's goal. In the early spring of 1895, soon after passing out of Sandhurst, he was commissioned second lieutenant in the 4th Hussars. For him, the next five years exceeded *'in vividness, variety and exertion anything I have known – except of course the opening months of the Great War'*. Impatient for action – and as he had had military training, that meant military action – he looked around his world. Victoria, Queen and Empress, was upon the throne; the British Empire spread far and wide across the world, and for the moment all was peace across the Empire.

It was not to be long before some corners of the Empire would offer *'little titbits of fighting'* to satisfy Churchill's restless nature, but the latter part of 1895 had nothing for him except a prolonged period of leave. He now found he could not afford all the pleasures life had to offer: *'Then as regards the Polo ponies,'* he had written to his mother in April, *'I have practised on other people's ponies for 10 days and am improving very fast. If therefore, as I imagine – you have some ready money, do lend me a hundred pounds – even if you do not think you will be able to give it to me as you said.'* Whether she did help him out is unclear – but he does record in *My Early Life* that by the time he came to be on leave he had spent all his money on polo ponies.

Then a *'little titbit'* presented itself – not in a British colony, but in the Spanish colony of Cuba, which had a history of bouts of insurrection. After nearly two decades of relative peace, Cuban guerrillas (supported by the United States) were mounting a new revolt against their Spanish rulers. On the basis that it would be good experience of warfare, Churchill and another young officer from the 4th Hussars managed to get permission to go to Cuba to observe the fighting at first hand; they were not to fight except in self-defence. Perhaps to give himself a little income, perhaps to put himself, ever so slightly, before the public eye, he came to an agreement with the *Daily Graphic* newspaper to send it articles on Cuba. These were to earn him compliments from the Manager of the *Daily Graphic,* and assurances that they were read and enjoyed by many, while a Lieutenant Craig-Brown, based in Jamaica, wrote congratulating him on them and enviously describing himself *'sitting in the mess-stores, totting up accounts and arranging menus while you are gaining experience & renown in the next island'*. Churchill was also to receive a letter from the British Ambassador to Spain, Sir Henry Drummond Wolff, asking him to tone down his criticisms of the Spanish: 'I am reproached for the unfavourable commentaries you make.' He was definitely beginning to make his mark.

On their arrival on the 'Pearl of the Antilles', the young officers had been welcomed by the Spanish authorities with warmth and hospitality; and soon found themselves marching with a Spanish column, occasionally coming under fire. *'To travel thousands of miles with money one could ill afford, and get up at four o'clock in the morning in the hope of getting into a scrape in the company of perfect strangers, is certainly hardly a rational proceeding,'* Churchill wrote in *My Early Life* – echoing, some thirty-five years later, a newspaper's comment that 'sensible people will wonder what motive could possibly impel a British officer to mix himself up in a dispute with the merits of which he had absolutely nothing to do . . . Spending a holiday in fighting other peoples' battles is rather an extraordinary proceeding even for a Churchill.'

Whatever the arguments, the experience contributed to the wide-ranging education that Churchill was now embarking on acquiring for himself. He saw the loveliness and felt the discomfort of the beautiful island; he gained a taste for cigars – which were to become his trademark ('the man with the big cigar' as the Second World War song was to go) – and for the afternoon siesta. Perhaps most important, he discovered that other nations – nations such as Spain – felt the same about their country and their colonies as the British felt about theirs. He thought this *'rather cheek'*, coming from foreigners, but acknowledged it and *'put it in my mental larder'*.

Another, lesser, aspect of his education was what the Spanish commanding officer's aide-de-camp called 'runcotelle', a drink he found *'extremely good'* but which it was many years before he learned was a rum cocktail.

There are many stories about Churchill's liking for drink and much speculation as to whether or not he was an 'alcohol abuser' or 'alcohol dependent'. There is no doubt that he liked alcoholic drinks – at first it was wine he liked, red and white, *'and especially champagne'*; occasionally brandy, but it was only while at Nowshera, on the North-West Frontier, with the Malakand Field Force, that he – apparently forcing himself to overcome a repugnance to it – acquired a taste for whisky, which was used to flavour the tepid water they had to drink (he later claimed to the last of his Private Secretaries, Anthony Montague Browne, that it was in South Africa that he learned to like it).

'I had been brought up and trained to have the utmost contempt for people who get drunk,' he wrote in *My Early Life*, although, he went on to write, he'd become more *'charitably'* inclined towards such frailties. Nevertheless he claimed that he himself had always practised *'true temperance'* – presumably meaning moderation, not abstinence. Certainly, claims that he drank very heavily seem to have been exaggerated – not least by himself, perhaps because it suited him from time to time to give the impression that he was the worse for drink, that his brain was perhaps not working as keenly as it actually was . . . In addition, the slurred Ss of his speech could have given the impression to those who did not know about this slight impediment that he was drunk. There are in fact few accounts of drunkenness; the most famous must be the exchange, in 1946, between him and Bessie Braddock, MP – a stout lady, to put it politely – as he was leaving the Commons bar: 'Winston,' she said icily, as he staggered into her, 'you're drunk.'

He drew himself up: *'Madam, you're ugly. But tomorrow I shall be shober.'*

In fact, according to his bodyguard, Ron Golding, who was with him at the time, Churchill was not drunk, just tired and shaky. His mind was certainly sharp enough to come up with a witty, if rude and malicious, retort.

Another Bessie Braddock story comes from Lord Carrington, who, not long after the Second World War became a whip in the House of Lords:

> One day Churchill, as party leader, came to lunch with the Tory whips; I looked at him in awe. He was either bored or in a bad temper or both. During the first two courses he never spoke. Then in came Bessie Braddock. Churchill looked up and said, '*Ah, there goes that constipated Britannia.*' He was so pleased with this remark that he became a different person.

Claims and counter-claims about Churchill's drinking abound. In 1942, the diplomat Lord Harvey remarked that 'He had beer, three ports and three brandies for lunch today, and has done it for years.' And Sir Ian Jacob of the wartime Defence Staff claimed of Churchill: 'He always had a bottle of champagne for lunch.' John Peck, one of Churchill's Private Secretaries, however, pointed out that Ian Jacob had rarely had lunch with Churchill, and that in any case Churchill himself only ever had a glass or two – the rest of the bottle would go elsewhere.

Also cited as proof is that after Churchill had been hit by a car in January 1932 in New York, Dr Otto C. Pickhardt wrote in a prescription for him: 'the use of alcoholic spirits at meal times . . . the minimum requirement to be 250 cc.' This does seem rather strange – perhaps, as it was still the Prohibition, Churchill had asked the doctor to prescribe alcohol as a kind of insurance in case he found himself among determinedly anti-alcohol society. He might have been remembering a couple of incidents that had occurred in 1929.

In Richmond, he had caused a bit of an upset at the home of Governor Harry Byrd, where he was staying. Unaware that Virginia was 'dry', he had asked for brandy. Byrd called a friend of his, John Stewart Bryan, and asked him if he could, as a matter of urgency, lay hands on a bottle; this was not easy, but Bryan managed to rush a bottle to the Governor. The next night he had to get another bottle. As Churchill was driven away at the end of his visit, Mrs Byrd turned to her husband. 'Harry,' she said, 'I don't know much about Mr Churchill, but I hope you won't invite him to this house again.'

In British Columbia, in Canada, he also ran up against the local liquor laws. He had been invited to address the Law Society at a dinner at a restaurant. Applications for a liquor licence had failed – there were to be no alcoholic drinks at the function.

On the afternoon of the dinner, the organizer of the event received a telephone call from Randolph Churchill who was accompanying his father: 'My father says if there are no drinks he won't come.' The organizer had gone to a lot of trouble over the dinner and lost his temper. 'You tell your father that if he doesn't come I will blacken his name right across Canada!' he said furiously and hung up. Arriving later at the chalet restaurant, he saw Churchill, calmly working at his easel. Churchill caught sight of him: *'It's all right,'* he said, patting a bulge in his jacket pocket, *'I've brought my own.'*

Cryptic statements like *'I have taken more out of alcohol than alcohol has taken out of me'*, and announcements such as '*No one can say that I ever failed to display a meet and proper appreciation of alcohol*' tended to bolster the tales that Churchill was a boozer – which he enjoyed encouraging. But there are signs, too, that his drinking – or the glass or bottle at his side – was part of the image he'd built himself. John Peck insisted, 'I *never* saw him the worse for drink. The glass of weak whisky, like the cigars, was more a symbol than anything else, and one glass lasted for hours.' Lord Hailes, also (as Patrick Buchan-Hepburn) a Private Secretary, said much the same: 'I never knew him to get drunk. He sipped coloured water all day, from morning to night: there was hardly any whisky in it at all.' While another Private Secretary, Sir David Hunt said, 'He certainly drank the weakest whisky-and-soda that I have ever known.' And Jock Colville described Churchill's usual tipple as 'more akin to mouthwash than a highball'. This was the drink Churchill's children dubbed 'Papa Cocktail': just enough whisky to cover the bottom of a tumbler, which was then filled with water and sipped throughout the morning. (He is supposed to have said – perhaps a bit irritably – to his son Randolph: '*Haven't you learned yet that I put something more than whisky into my speeches?*')

It would seem then that although Churchill enjoyed his drink, and could get through a huge amount during meals, his early training at Sandhurst – where officers were expected to know their limits and drunkenness was a deep disgrace – stayed with him. While he was working, the full glass by his hand was for show and mostly just water to quench his thirst – but water flavoured as he had come to like it in his early battlefield days in Malakand and South Africa. That he was dependent on spirits seems unlikely – he apparently won a bet with Lord Rothermere in 1936 that he could go without hard spirits for a year. No doubt he made up with wine – but here too it seems that his appreciation was *'meet and proper': 'A single glass of champagne imparts a feeling of exhilaration. The nerves are braced, the imagination is agreeably stirred, the wits become more nimble. A bottle produces the contrary effect. Excess causes a comatose insensibility.'* (And champagne was his favourite drink – it is said that during the Second World War, his friend Madame Pol-Roger, of the champagne house, kept two cases of vintage champagne for Churchill, which she had hidden from the Nazis.)

Above all, Churchill enjoyed teasing. *'When I was younger I made it a rule never to take strong drink before lunch. It is now my rule never to do so before breakfast,'* he once declared. While (as recorded in the sixth volume of *The Second World War*) on the occasion of a lunch with the Arab leader Ibn Saud, when he heard that the king's religion forbade drinking and smoking, he couldn't resist announcing: *'I must point out that my rule of life prescribes as an absolutely sacred rite smoking cigars and also the drinking of alcohol before, after, and if need be during all meals and in the intervals between them.'* (If this was to Ibn Saud's face, he must have made it clear he was joking.) And in 1946, sitting next to the Iraqi Ambassador Daud Pasha al-Haidari at a public banquet, he was heard to offer the Ambassador a glass of whisky. The invitation was politely declined on the grounds that the drinking of alcohol is prohibited by the Muslim religion. *'What, you don't drink? Good God! . . . I mean Jesus Christ . . . I mean Allah!'*

He was especially irritated by those who made a virtue of their temperance. When Field Marshal Montgomery said smugly, 'I neither drink nor smoke and am a hundred per cent fit,' Churchill was quick to retort: 'I *drink and smoke and I am* two *hundred per cent fit.'* He and Montgomery were to become good friends, but he never got on with Nancy Astor (the first woman to hold, though not to win, a seat in Parliament, which she retained from 1919 to 1945), who was, among other things, a champion of temperance. On one occasion Churchill had just stood up to address the House and was raising a glass of water to his lips when he caught sight of her. *'It must be a great pleasure for the noble lady,'* he boomed, *'. . . to see me drink water.'*

And when Churchill was First Lord of the Admiralty, he was approached by a temperance group with the suggestion that he reconsider the naval tradition of christening a ship by breaking a bottle of champagne across the bow as such a practice, they felt, added an undesirable glamour to champagne.

'But, madam,' Churchill replied to the group's spokeswoman, *'the hallowed custom of the Royal Navy is indeed a splendid example of temperance. The ship takes its first sip of wine and then proceeds on water ever after.'*

A frequently told story involves Churchill's friend Frederick Lindemann (who in 1941 was made 1st Viscount Cherwell), Professor of Experimental Philosophy (Physics) at Oxford, and describes a tableau that sounds like something of a party piece. Churchill greatly admired Lindemann's scientific brain, and sometimes when they were together in a roomful of people, he would glance round and say, loud enough for all to hear, *'Prof! Pray calculate the volume of champagne, whisky and other spirits I have consumed in my entire life and tell us how high it would reach if poured into this room.'*

Lindemann would then take out his slide rule and calculate (or pretend to) the necessary figures. Eventually, he would frown and say, 'I'm sorry, Winston, it would reach only to our ankles' (or 'knees' if it was a particularly small room). Churchill would give a sigh and say, *'How far to go . . . how little time remains.'*

Back in Britain, in 1895, there followed for Churchill some six months of 'idleness'. Much of that time was spent meeting (and pestering) people who would at some point in the future help in furthering his career (for instance, at a house party he persuaded General Sir Bindon Blood, in command of the troops on the North-West Frontier, to agree that he should allow him to join any future expedition there). He was to write, many years later, in *Painting as a Pastime*, *'The first quality that is needed is audacity';* for him this also applied to getting a foot on to the bottom rung, and the next, and the next, of the ladder of achievement.

A fair amount of time was spent playing polo: *'I want very much to buy another pony, I wish you would lend me £200 as I could then buy a really first-class animal which would always fetch his price,'* he again wrote to his mother. By the time his regiment was due to leave for India that autumn, he had five good ponies to sell.

On board ship the 4th Hussars began implementing a plan which meant that on disembarkation at Bombay in October 1896 they were able to buy twenty-five good, ready-trained polo ponies to take with them to

Bangalore, in order that they might not disgrace themselves on the polo field as newly arrived regiments, with untrained ponies, usually did. The plan was a success. In November they travelled to a tournament in Hyderabad, and won it. *'This performance is a record, no English regiment ever having won a first-class tournament within a month of their arrival in India,'* Churchill wrote triumphantly to his mother.

'Princes could live not better than we,' Churchill wrote of regimental life in Bangalore. Each day followed the same pattern, the highlight being *'the hour of Polo'.* Undemanding as this existence was – *'there is every tendency to relapse into a purely animal state of existence'* – it did not suit one whose resolve was to be a high-flier by *'notability or notoriety'.* With the care that he and his comrades had put into their strategy for achieving success on the polo field, he continued his self-imposed task of making himself into a force to be reckoned with. It was now time to compensate for some of the deficiencies in his education, he decided, and to read, read, read.

He detailed Lady Randolph to send books out to him and over the next months he read (*'three or four books at a time to avoid tedium'*), among others, Gibbon's eight-volume *Decline and Fall of the Roman Empire,* twelve volumes of Macaulay, works by Schopenhauer and Malthus, Darwin's *Origin of Species*, Plato's *Republic* (in translation, of course) Henry Fawcett's *Political Economy*, William Lecky's *European Morals* and *Rise and Influence of Rationalism,* Pascal's *Provincial Letters,* Adam Smith's *Wealth of Nations* and Hallam's *Constitutional History of England.*

He also asked his mother to send him all one hundred volumes of the *Annual Register*, the record of British public events, founded by Edmund Burke, as he wanted to know '*the detailed Parliamentary (debates, divisions, parties, cliques and caves) of the last one hundred years*'. Lady Randolph compromised by sending him the volumes that had appeared since his birth.

Bartlett's Familiar Quotations was a key tool in Churchill's self-education programme: '*It is a good thing for an uneducated man to read books of quotations,*' he wrote in *My Early Life*, somewhat sententiously ('*I suppress with difficulty an impulse to become sententious,*' he once said). He read it '*intently*', adding that '*the quotations when engraved upon the memory give you good thoughts*' as well as leading you to read the authors' works.

Winston Churchill is himself now among the most widely quoted authors and orators. Over the years he made good use of all the works he had read – quoting, borrowing, adapting the words of others for use in his writings and his speeches (for instance, '*iron curtain*', '*blood, sweat and tears*'). His memory was excellent – but, crowded as it was with phrases read or heard, coined or embellished, he did not always get it right. On one occasion he acknowledged he had made a mistake in quoting someone, and remarked, '*I am reminded of the professor who, in his declining hours, was asked by his devoted pupils for his final counsel. He replied, "Verify your quotations."*' Ironically, this itself is probably a misattribution: Churchill's likeliest source is a speech given in 1897 by the Earl of Rosebery (Prime Minister from 1894 to 1895), in which referred to 'the advice given by one aged sage to somebody who sought his guidance in life, namely, "Always wind up your watch and verify your quotations."' Who this aged professor/sage is remains uncertain, though it is thought that it might have been the Oxford professor Martin Joseph Routh, who advised 'verify your references' (well before his death in 1854).

Churchill also – understandably – re-used or adapted his own phrases where they were particularly felicitous. Perhaps he would have said, like George Bernard Shaw, the man he loved to hate: 'I often quote myself. It adds spice to my conversation.'

At the same time as attending to his education, Churchill was looking for other areas in which to advance himself. The army he saw as a step up to greater things – politics. *'It is a fine game to play,'* he wrote to his mother, *'the game of politics and it is well worth waiting for a good hand before really plunging.'* He bemoaned the fact that he was in India during a by-election: *'Had I been in England I might have contested it and should have won – almost to a certainty,'* he claimed with youthful extravagance in a letter to his mother. *'Instead of being an insignificant subaltern I should have had opportunities of learning those things which will be of value to me in the future.'* When it came to important political figures, the views Winston aired to his mother were adolescently arrogant. Balfour (First Lord of the Treasury) was *'languid, lazy, lack-a-daisical',* Curzon (Under-Secretary for Foreign Affairs) *'blown with conceit',* Salisbury (then Prime Minister for the third time, and the last to govern from the Lords) was *'able'* but *'obstinate* [and] *joins the brain of a statesman to the delicate susceptibilities of a mule'.* He was, nevertheless, to dedicate his third book, *The River War*, to Salisbury in most fulsome terms.

(A childish rudeness was to remain with him through his life, regularly exercised once he became a Member of Parliament when insults flew merrily to and fro across the floor. Some of his insults were truly infantile, even when he was far from childhood – of John Foster Dulles, the US Secretary of State, for instance, he said, *'Dull, duller, dulles'*. He could be more sophisticated, though. He commented of the stiffly upright Stafford Cripps, *'His chest is a cage in which two squirrels are at war – his conscience and his career.'* Of Clement Attlee he was to remark, *'If any grub is fed on Royal Jelly it turns into a queen bee';* and of his friend and Cabinet colleague Austen Chamberlain: *'He always played the game and he always lost it'*, while he continued to find fault with Balfour: *'If you wanted nothing done, Arthur Balfour was the best man for the task. There was no equal to him.'*)

When home on leave he did not cease from badgering people, and, with his mother's help, cultivating social and political contacts; and while he was in India Lady Randolph continued working on his behalf. *'She left no wire unpulled, no stone unturned, no cutlet uncooked.'* He very much wanted to accompany Kitchener's expedition to drive the religious leader, the Mahdi, and his dervish army (that, in 1885, had killed General Gordon) from the Sudan. *'Two years in Egypt my dearest Mamma – with a campaign thrown in – would I think qualify me to be allowed to beat my sword into a paper cutter and my sabretache into an election address.'*

In the summer of 1897 there came news of an uprising on the North-West Frontier. Churchill, on leave at the time, and having just given his first address at a political meeting, shot off straight away – it comes as no surprise that he *'only just caught the train'*. A long journey brought some disappointment: General Sir Bindon Blood was unable to give him a military appointment: 'no vacancies; come up as a correspondent; will try to fit you in.' Arrangements were made for Churchill's reports to appear in the local English paper, the *Pioneer*, and, back in Britain, in the *Daily Telegraph*.

'Nothing in life is so exhilarating as to be shot at without result'. So wrote Churchill in the fruit of this expedition – his first book, *The Malakand Field Force*. Although he was on the Indian frontier as a newspaper correspondent he did also take part in the action. At Harrow, Churchill claimed in *My Early Life*, instead of learning Latin and Greek, the *'stupidest boys'* were taught the English language through and through. *'Thus I got into my bones the essential structure of the ordinary British sentence – which is a noble thing.'* His ability with the English language stood him in good stead. The newspaper articles formed the basis of Churchill's first book, which (in spite of having been appallingly proofread by Lady Randolph's brother-in-law) was very well received.

On his return (with a campaign medal) to Bangalore, he resumed writing his only novel, *Savrola*; got himself appointed to a military expedition to Tirah but was disappointed to see no action, and continued to lobby everyone he could think of who might help him to take part in the Sudan campaign under General Sir Herbert Kitchener. The General did not like him ('publicity seeking', 'medal hunting' he considered Churchill), while Churchill remarked of him, *'He may be a general – but never a gentleman'*. It took the death of a subaltern in the 21st Lancers, and pressure from higher authority, for Kitchener to agree to take him on.

There was never any question as to young Winston Churchill's courage, but there was a kind of calculation in his pursuit of danger. *'I feel that the fact of having seen service with British troops while still a young man must give me more weight politically, must add to my claims to be listened to and may perhaps improve my prospects of gaining popularity with the country,'* he had written to his mother. *'Besides this, I think I am of an adventurous disposition and shall enjoy myself not so much in spite of as because of the risks I run.'*

And, a bit more sombrely, *'I mean to play this game out and if I lose it is obvious that I never could have won any other. The unpleasant contingency is one which could have permanent effects and would while leaving me life deprive me of all that makes life worth living.'*

With Kitchener's troops, he took part in the famous cavalry charge at Omdurman, where many of his companions died – over twenty per cent of the regiment. On the way home, Churchill experienced being *'flayed alive'* when he donated a piece of skin to patch a friend's wound. Many years later, Churchill recounts in *My Early Life*, he met Admiral David Beatty, who had watched the charge from a gunboat. Churchill asked him how it had looked to him: 'It looked like plum duff: brown currants scattered about in a great deal of suet.' Churchill himself, asked many years later, by Anthony Montague Browne how he had felt during the famous charge, replied, *'It was very stimulating, but I did think, "Suppose there is a spoil-sport in the hole with a machine-gun?"'*

He had proved himself in the army, and now decided

that a writing career – as a war correspondent and as the author of books (he was working on *The River War*, an account of Kitchener's campaign) – was *'more likely to assist me in pursuing the larger ends of life'* – i.e. politics.

In the summer of 1899 an opportunity presented itself in the shape of an election in Oldham, Lancashire, where he stood as a Conservative candidate. He enjoyed campaigning and making speeches, though he seems to have anticipated defeat, remarking in a letter to Pamela Plowden, whom he was courting in a rather vague way: *'And at each meeting I am conscious of growing powers and facilities of speech, and it is in this that I shall find my consolation should the result be, as is probable, unfortunate.'*

Defeat, he later wrote, left him feeling like a bottle of champagne or of soda that had been left to go flat. But trouble was soon fizzing up, this time in South Africa, for him to turn his restless attention to. *'England is a very great Power and the Boers are a miserably small people, and I ask how long is the peace of the country and the Empire going to be disturbed by a party of filibustering Boers,'* he proclaimed in a speech in August. (For the past century and more, South Africa had been torn apart by fighting between the earlier Dutch settlers, the Boers, and, first, the local Zulus; and then, later, British colonists. Relations were not good, and were worsening as large numbers of mostly British immigrants flooded into Boer territory. At issue between the Boers and the British was South Africa's rich mineral resources: the Boers were largely farmers; the immigrants were miners and prospectors, seeking gold and diamonds: unsurprisingly, they were resisted by the

Boers, who had farmed the land for, in some cases, centuries. The interests of the indigenous population, the Africans, received little consideration.)

With the start of the second Boer War in October 1899, Churchill, now out of the army, managed to secure an appointment as the *Morning Post's* special correspondent in South Africa. The *Dunottar Castle* set sail on 14 October; on board with Churchill were the Commander-in-Chief, South Africa, General Sir Redvers Buller and a number of staff officers, and an old friend of Lord Randolph's, Lord Gerard, who, now far from young, had been promised by Sir Redvers Buller that he might accompany him should he ever command an army in South Africa. (Gerard, according to Churchill, was given cases of champagne and brandy to take with him, which, apparently, he was to share with Churchill. Not wishing these cases to be plundered, Gerard labelled them 'castor oil'. A cunning plan, which backfired. Two months later, there was still no sign of them. On enquiring from the base as to their fate, Lord Gerard was told that they had been issued in error to the hospitals – but he was not to worry, there was plenty of castor oil at the base and a supply was on its way.)

An uncomfortable sea journey marked the start of the kind of adventures encountered by the 'Young Indiana Jones'. Although Churchill was appointed as a journalist the opportunity to take part in action was irresistible. When a friend from India days, Captain Haldane, invited him to accompany an armoured train he was commanding, Churchill jumped at the chance to gather information for the *Morning Post* and *'also because I was eager for trouble'.* In anticipation he took with him the Mauser he had had in Omderman. When the train came under fire from a raiding party of Boers under the command of Louis Botha (later a good friend), and was partially derailed, Churchill seems – fortunately – to have been too busy trying to right the wrecked carriages and help the wounded ('as brave a man as could be found,' one of them said), and to encourage the train driver to get the engine and part of the train back to safety, to make use of his pistol. Indeed, he had left it on the train, and thus avoided being killed when he was captured. He might have been released on the grounds that he was a non-combatant journalist but the British South African press made this impossible; referring in one instance to 'Lieutenant Churchill', local papers declared: 'but for his presence on the train, not a single Englishman or soldier would have escaped. After the train was forced to a standstill the officers and men would definitely have fallen into enemy hands had he not directed proceedings in such a clever and thorough way, whilst walking alongside the engine, that the train together with its load escaped capture.'

Churchill and Haldane were among those held at the State Model School, Pretoria. There Churchill passed his twenty-fifth birthday and there he, Haldane and a Sergeant Brockie planned an escape. In the event, only Churchill got away, climbing out *'of a public conven-ience, into world-wide acclaim and notoriety'*, as he put it. To add to the drama of his escape, after he had walked a few miles he leaped on to a moving goods train (providing wonderful copy for newspaper columnists and artists) and spent the night among coal sacks and jumped off some eighty miles on, making for Portuguese East Africa. By sheer luck he found an Englishman, who kept him hidden for a week, while the

Boers searched for him. The police commissioner sent out a letter asking to be informed without delay should he be seen – he was described as

an Englishman, 25 years of age, about 5 feet 8 inches in height, medium build, stooping gait, fair complexion, reddish brown hair, almost invisible slight moustache, speaks through his nose, cannot give full expression to the letter 's', and does not know a word of Dutch. Wore a suit of brown clothes, but not uniform – an ordinary suit of clothes.

A poster offered 'vijf en twintig pond stg.' (£25 sterling) for his recapture. But he was not caught. Another long freight-train journey and a boat trip took him to Durban, where he received a hero's welcome. (Interestingly, he said of the Boers to his colleague John Atkins, the *Manchester Guardian* correspondent, *'They have the better cause – and the cause is everything – at least, I mean to them it is a better cause.'*)

Impressed, General Buller took Churchill on as a nominal member of the South Africa Light Horse (since Churchill's despatches from Omdurman, the War Office had prohibited men from holding the dual position of soldier and correspondent, but Buller managed to get round this). Churchill threw himself into action with gusto and a great deal of courage. He wrote to Pamela Plowden that he would not leave Africa until the matter was settled: *'I should forfeit my self-respect for ever if I tried to shield myself like that behind an easily obtained reputation for courage. No possible advantage politically could compensate – besides believe me none would result . . . but I have a good belief that I am to be of some use and therefore to be spared.'*

He was in the first relief column to arrive, in February 1900, to end the siege at Ladysmith, where, incidentally, a Captain Gilfilan overheard an officer ask General Sir George White, 'Who on earth is that?' to receive the reply, 'That's Randolph Churchill's son Winston; I don't like the fellow, but he'll be Prime Minister of England one day.'

On more than one occasion Churchill came within a hair's-breadth of being killed; in an earlier letter to his mother, from the Sudan, he had referred to *'my luck in these things'*; he then came to believe that he was *'to be preserved for future things'*, as he wrote to his mother. At Spion Kop, he wrote to Pamela Plowden, where *'the scenes . . . were among the strangest and most terrible I have ever witnessed'*, he spent five days under continual shell and rifle fire, and *'once the feather on my hat was cut through by a bullet'*.

There was also discomfort, as he wrote in *My Early Life*:

The night was chilly. Colonel Byng and I shared a blanket. When he turned over I was in the cold. When I turned over I pulled the blanket off him and he objected. He was the Colonel. It was not a good arrangement.

On another occasion, the cavalry were trying to take a small hill from a group of Boer horsemen, Churchill had just dismounted when they came under fire and his mount fled; dodging the bullets, he ran towards his men and was scooped up by a trooper, who might well by this action have saved Churchill's life. Unfortunately, the bullets struck his horse, which fell, dying. 'Oh my poor horse,' lamented the trooper, according to

Randolph Churchill. *'Never mind,'* Churchill tried to console him. *'You've saved my life.'* 'But it's the horse I'm thinking about,' the young man said sadly. (He was later awarded the Distinguished Conduct Medal for his heroic act.)

Among reported acts of derring-do was a bicycle ride through Boer-occupied Johannesburg carrying despatches from Colonel Ian Hamilton to Field Marshal Lord Roberts, Buller's replacement. He was one of two cyclists – and he was the one who was taken to see the Field Marshal. This was followed by a moment of glory, when Churchill (with his cousin the Duke of Marlborough, Colonel Hamilton's ADC) rode with the first column into Pretoria. He hurried to the POW camp: 'suddenly Winston Churchill came galloping over the hill and tore down the Boer flag, and hoisted ours amidst cheers, and our people, some of which had been in for six months or more, were free and at once the Boer guards were put inside and our prisoners guard over them! It was roarable and splendid,' wrote one of the newly liberated prisoners.

A month later, in June 1900, came a British victory at Diamond Hill. Ian Hamilton wrote in his memoirs: 'Winston gave the embattled hosts at Diamond Hill an exhibition of conspicuous gallantry for which he has never received full credit.'

'I need not say how anxious I am to come back to England. Politics, Pamela, finances and books all need my attention,' Churchill had written to his mother – perhaps somewhat self-importantly – shortly before the battle of Diamond Hill, and it was not long before he did return to England, setting sail, once more on the *Dunottar Castle*, on 20 July 1900.

He arrived in Britain to find himself famous, a hero. Another two books were published; and a lecture tour on his experiences helped his finances. Politics he was working on all the time, and Pamela slid out of his life and married someone else. A well-timed by-election at Oldham gave him the coveted seat in Parliament.

Chapter 3

The Glow-worm

H E HAD ACHIEVED his first step to the top. Now that he had a seat in Parliament he could begin to have some influence in the running of his country. *'I was twenty-six,'* Churchill wrote in *My Early Life. 'Was it wonderful that I should have thought I had arrived? But luckily life is not so easy as all that: otherwise we should get to the end too quickly.'* He tried to cultivate his moustache – the one remarked upon by the Boer Police Commissioner – to lend him an appearance of greater maturity and dignity, befitting to a Member of Parliament. Not long after, a woman came up to him, and said forthrightly: 'There are two things I don't like about you, Mr Churchill – your politics and your moustache.' He was not, however, at a loss for a satisfying retort: *'My dear madam,'* he replied, *'pray do not disturb yourself. You are not likely to come into contact with either.'*

It is said that while Churchill was canvassing during his 1900 campaign a member of the electorate exclaimed: 'Vote for you? Why, I'd rather vote for the Devil!' *'I understand,'* Churchill answered. *'But in case your friend is not running, may I count on your support?'* This kind of mental and verbal agility served him well over the next decades in the House of Commons. And those decades were certainly to be a roller-coaster ride for him, one in which he rubbed many people up the wrong way, charmed and stirred many people, quarrelled with many, made a number of rash decisions – and, ultimately, played a crucial part in saving his country, and much of the rest of the world, from a sorry fate. It was probably just as well that the Devil didn't get elected. Many years later, however, Churchill did remark, *'If Hitler invaded hell I would make at least a favourable reference to the Devil in the House of Commons.'*

Given his military background, it is unsurprising that Churchill's maiden speech was about the Boer War, and that he started parliamentary life by busying himself with matters of army reform and economy. Indeed, a mere stripling of an MP, he had the effrontery to criticize his own party's overspending on the army, objecting, in May 1901, to the suggestion of having a total of three army corps, and in so doing painting a sombre view of what might come. The army, he told the Commons,

> *ought to be reduced by two army corps, on the grounds that one is quite enough to fight savages, and three are not enough even to begin to fight Europeans . . . A European war cannot be anything but a cruel, heartrending struggle, which, if we are ever to enjoy the bitter fruits of victory, must demand, perhaps for several years, the whole manhood of the nation, the entire*

suspension of peaceful industries, and the concentrating to one end of every vital energy in the community . . . a European war can only end in the ruin of the vanquished and the scarcely less fatal commercial dislocation and the exhaustion of the conquerors. Democracy is more vindictive than Cabinets. The wars of peoples will be more terrible than those of kings.

This was startlingly prescient, in line with Churchill's belief that he was being *'preserved'* for some future event. Questioned at the time he might have said, as he did elsewhere, *'Study history, study history. In history lie all the secrets of statecraft,'* and *'The farther back you can look, the farther forward you are likely to see.'*

He found himself disagreeing with the Conservative government over other matters – the plight of the poverty-stricken, for instance (he was much affected by Seebohm Rowntree's book on the poor of York). He 'crossed the floor' to join the Liberal Opposition in May 1904. Challenged in the 1906 election, in which he stood as the Liberal parliamentary candidate for Manchester North-West, about the anti-Liberal stance he had taken, and anti-Liberal views he had propounded, as a Conservative, he gave the sanctimonious-sounding reply: *'I said a lot of stupid things when I was in the Conservative party, and I left it because I did not want to go on saying stupid things.'*

He won the seat. Arthur Balfour, now Conservative Prime Minister, must have felt that his 1899 remark about Churchill had been only too true: 'I thought he was a young man of promise; but it appears he is a young man of promises.' But to Churchill the important promises had been those to his conscience, to his principles – although perhaps also with a nod to his ambition. Crossing over to the Opposition does not seem to be a clever career move, when the Opposition party has been weak and divided for some years. So perhaps it was indeed a matter of principle. On the other hand, the Liberals were now beginning to show a strong united front . . . So did Churchill foresee their forthcoming success?

Words such as 'truth', 'lies', 'conscience', 'principle', and so on, are bandied about all too often in the speech of politicians – Churchill characterized the average parliamentary candidate thus: *'He is asked to stand, he wants to sit, he is expected to lie.'* These are the people for whom *'A change of party is usually considered a much more serious breach of consistency than a change of view'.* Was he one of those? Or was he prepared to sacrifice his position for the sake of principle? Certainly, with neat one-liners like *'Some men change their party for the sake of their principles; others their principles for the sake of their party',* it is clear that that is what he wanted people to believe. But it is what he too believed, while he was probably fairly sure that he would – possibly with the help of his principles – regain that position. (That belief again – that he was destined for some great thing; fortunately he never went as far as suggesting, one hopes even thinking, that his destiny was to save mankind.)

He revealed at times a passionate concern for the value of conscience and of truth (which he was careful to distinguish from honesty), even when making witty comments at the expense of other politicians. In 1940, on the death of Neville Chamberlain, Churchill was to say in a generous tribute to the man whom he had, only a few months earlier, succeeded as Prime Minister, *'The only guide to a man is his conscience; the only shield to his memory is the rectitude and sincerity of his actions. It is very imprudent to walk through life without this shield.'*

On another occasion he declared that *'The truth is incontrovertible. Panic may resent it; ignorance may deride it; malice may distort it, but there it is.'* The trouble was, he felt, that even when the truth *was* there, it was studiously ignored: he once observed of Stanley Baldwin that he occasionally *'stumbled over the truth, but hastily picked himself up and hurried on as if nothing had happened.'* Baldwin, however, adhered to honesty, but was not necessarily able to perceive the broader truth: *'It is a fine thing to be honest, but it is also very important to be right,'* Churchill pointed out. (Interestingly, Baldwin said of Churchill that he 'cannot really tell lies. That is what makes him so bad a conspirator', while Balfour remarked to Churchill upon 'the exaggerated way you tell the truth'.)

Churchill was to say, in 1943, *'Sometimes truth is so precious, it must be attended by a bodyguard of lies.'* (He was at the Tehran Conference, and was referring specifically to European invasion plans.) He took the pragmatic view, as illustrated by the following story related by Sir Anthony Montague Browne. During the Blitz (1940–1) one of the heads of London's transport services refused to put his name to a statement that in spite of an enemy air attack the London transport services were running normally. Churchill, then Prime Minister, was convinced that to keep up people's morale, the authorities should give assurances that all was running as normal. The official in question said simply –

and reasonably – 'It's just not true.' Churchill sent for him and reasoned with him at length, but in vain. The man was all too sea-green. Eventually Churchill dismissed him: *'I will do violence to no man's conscience,'* he said wearily, adding, after the man had gone from the room, *'And never let me see that impeccable bus conductor again.'*

Some years after he had left Balfour's government, and while serving under Asquith, the Liberal Prime Minister, Churchill produced another nice distinction: *'Balfour,'* he said, *'is wicked and moral. Asquith is good and immoral.'*

In 1906 Churchill met Violet Asquith, daughter of Herbert Asquith, then Chancellor of the Exchequer. She was later to recall him earnestly expounding to her at length upon life, the human race and its potential, and ending with the words, *'We are all worms. But I do believe I am a glow-worm.'*

On getting home she told her father that she 'had seen genius'. 'Winston would certainly agree with you there,' she recollected him replying, 'but I am not sure whether you will find many others of the same mind. Still, I know exactly what you mean. He is not only remarkable but unique.'

With the Liberal victory in the 1906 election, the new Liberal MP was appointed Under-Secretary of State for the Colonies, in which role he proceeded to get up a number of people's noses. Lord Elgin, the Secretary of State for the Colonies – his immediate boss – found him something of a trial: 'When I accepted Churchill as my Under-Secretary, I knew I should have no easy task,' he was to write. Sir Francis Hopwood, Permanent Under-Secretary, wrote to Elgin that Churchill 'is most tiresome . . . The restless energy, the uncontrollable desire for notoriety and the lack of moral perception make him an anxiety indeed.' When Churchill presented Elgin with a list of suggestions – being somewhat opinionated, he had many – with the note *'These are my views. W. S. C.'*, Elgin added, 'But not mine. E.' Lady Lugard (Flora Shaw), the knowledgeable and distinguished wife of the Governor of Hong Kong, was of the opinion that Churchill was 'an ignorant boy, so obviously ignorant in regard to colonial affairs and at the same time so full of personal activity that the damage he may do appears to be colossal.' And when Churchill visited Africa, the Governor of Uganda complained that Churchill was 'a perfect nuisance, dodging about with his camera all the time'.

When he lost his Manchester seat in 1908, the Conservatives cheered – but he popped up and won the Liberal seat in Dundee that same year. He now alarmed and annoyed many by advocating radical social reforms; Charles Masterman, a fellow Liberal, was disparaging: 'He is full of the poor, whom he has just discovered. He thinks he is called by providence to do something for them.'

Churchill did do something, at least: as President of the Board of Trade in 1909 and 1910, he set up the first Labour Exchanges. In 1910, as Home Secretary, he put in place major reforms to prisons, which led to the writer John Galsworthy remarking to Lady Randolph's sister, 'I have always admired his pluck and his capacity, I now perceive him to have a heart and to be very warm.'

*

In 1908, Winston Churchill married Clementine Hozier, which, in terms of finances, was not a good match as she was not rich – indeed she earned a bit of pin-money by giving French lessons. She was good-looking, serious, sensitive and well educated. Some of Churchill's women friends, friends of hers, were none too pleased: 'stupid as an owl . . . Father thinks that it spells disaster for them both . . . she is sane to the point of dreariness,' Violet Asquith wrote to Venetia Stanley, her father's lover, while the latter wrote 'I wonder how stupid Winston thinks her.' Clementine was very far from stupid, however, and the marriage was very far from a disaster. It endured all the ups and downs of Churchill's political career, and, as the many very affectionate letters between them (between Winston, 'Pug' or 'Pig', and Clemmie, 'Cat' or 'Kat') testify, so did their love. Asked what he considered his most brilliant achievement, Churchill replied that it was to *'persuade my wife to marry me'*. On another occasion, the question 'If you could not be who you are, who would you like to be?' was making the round of the dinner table; eventually it was Churchill's turn, and everybody waited expectantly to hear what the great former wartime prime minister would say. *'If I could not be who I am, I would most like to be . . .'* he paused for effect, then, turning to Clementine: *'Mrs Churchill's second husband.'*

The often-cited words, *'My wife and I tried two or three times in the last forty years to have breakfast together, but it was so disagreeable we had to stop'*, from a 1950 letter to an American friend need not be taken to suggest any fundamental falling-out between the two of them – quite simply, Clementine probably preferred to get up for breakfast, while Churchill stayed late in bed, breakfasting there, and working, even conducting meetings from his bed, often in the company of a dog, cat or bird. R. A. Butler, as Minister for Education, on a visit to Chequers in 1943, found the Prime Minister in bed, with Nelson the cat curled up on his feet: *'This cat,'* declared Churchill, *'does more for the war effort than you do. He acts as a hot-water bottle and saves fuel and power.'* A couple of years before, however, Churchill had had to reprove his hot-water bottle for deserting him when air-raid sirens sounded: *'Nelson, think of your namesake – no one named Nelson slinks under a bed in a time of crisis.'*

The rows between Clementine and Winston were often public and droll enough not to be serious. Churchill's last Private Secretary, Anthony Montague Browne tells of how, after a disagreement with her husband, Clementine swept out of the room saying in a quiet voice, 'Winston, I have been married to you for forty-five years for better – ' then, loudly – 'AND FOR WORSE!' At which Churchill looked at his Private Secretary 'silently for a moment and then observed solemnly: *"I am the most unhappy of men."* This was so manifestly absurd,' continues Montague Browne, 'that I could not help bursting into an unseemly peal of laughter, which W. S. C. did not seem to mind.' It was not just absurd – it was patently untrue.

There is even a story – if true, surely exaggerated – that some time during Churchill's first premiership, the Archbishop of Canterbury called upon him unexpectedly and was more than a little startled when he walked into the room to find Mr and Mrs Churchill both on all fours on the floor, saying 'oink, oink' and 'meow' to each other.

They were to have five children, one of whom was to die at the age of three.

Churchill's time as Home Secretary exposed him to new experiences. It coincided, for instance, with a growth in the movement towards women's suffrage. His Victorian childhood had taught him that at home (and sometimes at schools for young children) the women ruled – the men attended to politics, war and business. He probably couldn't really understand why women should want the vote (it was not in keeping with his view of women's role in society), but could not see any reason why they should not have it, and when he had joined the Liberals he supported *'the strong current of evolution'* which would give women the vote. Unfortunately, during his 1906 campaign in Manchester (home of the Pankhursts), he had run up against the more militant of the suffragettes. Irritated by their constant heckling, and disapproving of rowdyism in women, he got up on his (metaphorical) high horse, and when asked how he would vote on the issue should he be elected, he rather pompously replied, *'The only time I have voted in the House of Commons on this question I have voted in favour of women's suffrage, but, having regard to the perpetual disturbance at public meetings, I utterly decline to pledge myself.'* He proceeded to make matters worse when, confronted by an angry crowd of women, he pronounced, perhaps out of a self-righteous fit of pique, *'Nothing would induce me to vote for giving women the franchise. I am not going to be henpecked into a question of such importance.'*

This was not wise and their hackles rose, but he was

not yet seen as the suffragettes' sworn enemy. When his engagement to Clementine was announced, a telegram arrived: 'Hearty congratulations on engagement have great hopes of your speedy conversion but you said you would not be henpecked A Manchester suffragette.'

Clementine was herself a suffragist (as distinct from a suffragette), advocating votes for women, but not participating in rallies and protest marches, and disapproving of the violence displayed by some of the more active suffragettes. Churchill was again coming round to the idea of supporting votes for women, writing *'I am anxious to see women relieved in principle from a disability which is injurious to them,'* when in 1910 he found himself confronted by an angry mob, and, so the story goes, had to be rescued by his wife from being pushed under a train at Bristol's Temple Meads station. His unusual indecisiveness – Mr Churchill, ran the newspaper report, was 'of opinion that the sex disqualification was not a true or logical disqualification, and he was therefore in favour of the principle of women being enfranchised. But he declined utterly to pledge himself to any particular bill . . .' – did nothing to warm the suffragettes to him.

He made himself further unpopular with them when as Home Secretary he allowed the police to deal unduly roughly with deputations of suffragettes sent to demonstrate outside Parliament in November 1910. It was not until 1918 that women over the age of thirty were given the vote, and another ten years before the franchise was extended to those over twenty-one. (In 1960, a reporter from the London *Evening Standard* asked Churchill what he thought about the prediction recently made that by the year 2000 women would be ruling the world. The reply was a wry *'They still will, will they?'*)

A different kind of social unrest, also in November 1910, brought him into more political hot water when, once again, Churchill deployed the police and seemed unable to keep them under control. This time it was at a miners' riot in the Welsh town of Tonypandy. Two men – said to have been innocent bystanders – were killed. He came in for much criticism from the left and the right, and the incident stuck in people's minds, over-shadowing, for instance, his Mines Act of 1911, which improved safety in the pits.

A couple of months later he made headline news again, when the allure of the battle front was too much for him and he could not resist joining the police and a troop of armed soldiers at a siege in Sidney Street, Stepney, where three or more armed, supposedly Latvian, robbers, who had already killed two policemen and wounded one, were holed up. A third policeman was killed, and another wounded. The house was then set on fire, and Churchill told the chief fire officer to let it burn. Although against the principles of the fire brigade, he *'thought it better to let the house burn down rather than spend good British lives in rescuing those ferocious rascals'*. If not just the villains, but firemen also, had been killed, he would have come under a greater storm of criticism. Commenting in the Commons on news-paper photographs showing the Home Secretary in the danger zone, the leader of the Conservatives, Balfour, said dryly, 'I understand what the photographer was doing, but what was the Right Honourable gentleman doing?'

To Charles Masterman, Churchill said, *'Don't be*

cross. It was such fun.' But, in a more serious vein, he did recognize that *'I should have done much better to have remained quietly in my office'*.

In 1935, he was to tell a *News of the World* journalist, *'Of all the offices I have held this was the one that I liked the least.'*

Chapter 4

The Dreadnought

IN 1909 Lloyd George, who was then Chancellor of the Exchequer, and Winston Churchill had resisted calls to equip the Navy with six dreadnoughts, insisting that four of these heavily armed battleships would suffice. A compromise was reached – four now, another four later should the need arise. Admiral Sir John Fisher, First Sea Lord until 1910, acknowledging the political power of the two men, suggested jokingly that the dreadnoughts be named 'No. 1. *Winston*, No. 2. *Churchill*, No. 3. *Lloyd*, No. 4. *George*. How they would fight! Uncircumventable!'

In 1911, a German gunboat appeared off the Moroccan coast; this concerned both the French and the British, who now suspected that the Germans presented a clear threat, and not just to France's interests in North Africa. Churchill now began to involve himself more in military and naval matters. Then Asquith – perhaps because he realized that nothing would stop his Home Secretary from meddling in defence issues – offered Churchill the position of First Lord of the Admiralty. Churchill was elated: *'This is a big thing – the biggest thing that has ever come my way – the chance I should have chosen before all others. I shall pour into it everything I've got.'*

True to form, Churchill managed to annoy a number of people. He made himself familiar – and interfered with – every aspect of the job; sacked and recruited officers as he (but not everyone else) saw fit; and he began to modernize and strengthen the Navy. Enthusiastically embracing new technology – as he once said, *'Unless the intellect of a nation keeps abreast of all material improvements, the society in which that occurs is no longer progressing'* – he was one of the first to see the military potential of aircraft, and in 1912 instituted the Royal Naval Air Service (even taking flying lessons, which he loved, but eventually had to give up to soothe an anxious Clementine), and established an Air Department at the Admiralty to make full use of this new technology. Generally, he was preparing for war – a memorandum he wrote in the summer of 1911 set out his view of how a war with Germany would evolve and develop, which was a chillingly prescient scenario as it turned out, but at the time it was seen as little more than an exaggerated interest in warfare.

From having wanted to cut spending on the Army and Navy, now Churchill wanted to increase it, and he was not going to take demurral quietly. In his diary for 1912, the Chancellor of the Duchy of Lancaster Charles Hobhouse made such statements as: 'Churchill is ill-mannered, boastful, unprincipled, without any redeeming qualities except his amazing ability and industry', and when a proposed increase in Army pay was reduced in November, 'We had the usual display of bad manners and bad temper . . . he stormed, sulked, interrupted. Like an ill-bred cub.'

Ramsay MacDonald, Chairman of the relatively new

Labour Party, which was still some way from being a significant Opposition party, wrote in 1913, 'Mr Churchill is a very dangerous person to put at the head of either of our fighting services. He treats them as hobbies.' Of MacDonald, Churchill was to remark, '*We know that he has, more than any other man, the gift of compressing the largest amount of words into the smallest amount of thought.*'

It was perhaps more that Churchill had a good nose for approaching war. Having himself been in the midst of fighting, he had no illusions as to what it entailed, and had said not long before, in a letter to his wife, '*Much as war attracts me and fascinates my mind with its tremendous situations – I feel more deeply every year – and can measure the feeling here in the midst of arms – what vile and wicked folly and barbarism it all is.*'

Now he wrote to her: '*Everything tends towards catastrophe and collapse. I am interested, geared up and happy. Is it not horrible to be built like that? The preparations have a hideous fascination for me . . . Yet I would do my best for peace, and nothing would induce me wrongfully to strike the blow.*'

There were lighter moments: at a diplomatic reception, an Italian military attaché asked a Luxembourgeois diplomat about a medal he was wearing. 'It is an ancient order called the Royal Admiralty Cross,' the diplomat replied stiffly. After he had stalked off, the Italian turned to the First Lord of the Admiralty and remarked how odd it was that Luxembourg should have this when it did not even have a navy. '*Why shouldn't they have an admiralty?*' Churchill answered cheerfully. '*You in Italy, after all, have a minister of finance – yet you don't have a treasury!*'

With the outbreak of war in 1914, Churchill, the Cabinet at the time dominated by the issue of Irish Home Rule, threw himself into it with gusto. *'We did not enter upon this war with the hope of easy victory . . . the war will be long and sombre,'* he said, echoing his words of thirteen years before, *'. . . we must derive from our cause and the strength that is in us, and from the traditions and history of our race, and from the support and aid of our Empire, the means to make our British plough go over obstacles of all kinds and continue to the end of the furrow, whatever the toil and suffering may be.'*

But soon he ran into further hot water. As usual, he could not resist having a hand in everything that was going on. He set up a new unit, the Royal Naval Division (naval, but to fight on land), which, just weeks after its formation he sent with the Royal Marines in response to a request from the Belgian government to help defend the port of Antwerp. Believing, perhaps, that he would be able to persuade the Belgians to hold out, Churchill joined his troops. Where command had to be taken, he was more than prepared to step into the breach. In *Front Everywhere* (1935), a memoir of the First World War, J. M. N. Jeffries recalls a huge traffic jam as the troops fell back on the city before the German advance, with everywhere a confusion of lorries, cars, horses, carts and people, milling about in every direction and effectively stopping dead all movement. No one did anything until a man jumped out of a car and up on to some handy elevation. 'There was some purpose in his gestures and power in his voice, and under his direction cars and carts were unlocked from each other and the traffic gradually sorted out into streams. The car in which I was seated fell into its own channel and went past with the others, but as

I looked back, he was still at his post, poised like a statue, watching till the order he had created was installed with durable momentum. It was Mr Winston Churchill.'

But the German forces overwhelmed them, British troops had to retreat, some taken prisoner, Antwerp surrendered, and Churchill returned to Britain and admonishment. 'He is not . . . a Napoleon, but a Minister of the Crown, with no time either to organize, or to lead armies in the field,' declared a newspaper.

There were enough problems at home – trouble was brewing in Ireland, and, closer still, among his colleagues. The First Sea Lord, Admiral Prince Louis of Battenberg, resigned in the face of a press campaign against him because of his German connections (he soon anglicized his name to Mountbatten), and Churchill recalled from retirement Admiral Fisher to take his place. Jackie Fisher and Field Marshal Lord Kitchener, Secretary of State for War, could not get on; General Sir John French, Commander-in-Chief of the BEF, could not get on with Kitchener. Fisher and Churchill, old friends that they were, were in constant disagreement. The following year, 1915, brought another disaster – a failed attempt to storm the Dardanelles by 'ships alone' in an effort to knock Turkey out of the war by seizing Constantinople. From the start the plan faced opposition: 'His volatile mind is at present set on Turkey and Bulgaria, and he wants to organize a heroic adventure against Gallipoli and the Dardanelles: to which I am altogether opposed,' Asquith wrote to Venetia Stanley.

The planned naval bombardment – which apparently was originally Fisher's idea and one that Churchill was initially none too certain about – was a sorry failure, and when Kitchener did send in troops it was too late; the Australian and New Zealand Army Corps followed on, but in some of the grimmest fighting of the war, the Turks held on – just – to the Peninsula, keeping the Allies back. Casualties were high, as were recriminations. In 1930, Churchill wrote (referring specifically to his first electoral defeat at Oldham in 1899, but clearly not only to that occasion), *'Everyone threw the blame on me. I have noticed that they nearly always do. I suppose it is because they think I shall be able to bear it best.'*

The Conservatives encouraged Asquith to order Churchill to resign. Instead, Churchill was given the post of Chancellor of the Duchy of Lancaster in a new Conservative-Liberal coalition government. 'The Dardanelles haunted him for the rest of his life . . . When he left the Admiralty he thought he was finished . . . I thought he would die of grief,' Clementine Churchill said much later.

Churchill felt *'Like a sea-beast fished up from the depths, or a diver too suddenly hoisted, my veins threatened to burst from the fall in pressure . . . At the moment when every fibre of my being was inflamed to action, I was forced to remain a spectator of the tragedy, placed cruelly in a front seat.'* To add insult to injury ideas that he had been working on for *'land battleships'* (tanks) were being scrapped – he had suggested to Asquith in January 1915 that it might be feasible to *'fit up a number of steam tractors with small armoured shelters, in which men and machine-guns could be placed, which would be bullet-proof . . . The caterpillar system would enable trenches to be crossed quite easily, and the weight of the machine would destroy all wire entanglements.'* Now it seemed as though these plans would never see the light of day.

After a few months – with never a chance to speak in the Commons – the desire for action resurfaced and Churchill resigned in order to go out to the Western Front: to find a major political figure in the trenches was unusual. On 18 November 1915 he rejoined the 4th Hussars as a major, and then with speed and efficiency got himself attached to the Grenadier Guards, before being appointed Lieutenant-Colonel commanding the 6th Royal Scots Fusiliers (an infantry battalion, although he was trained for the cavalry).

One soldier told *The Times* that 'a cooler and braver officer never wore the King's uniform . . . His coolness is the subject of much discussion among us, and everybody admires him.'

An Italian journalist was much impressed:

I was in the battle line near Lierre, and in the midst of a group of officers stood a man. He was still young, and was enveloped in a cloak, and on his head wore a yachtsman's cap. He was tranquilly smoking a large cigar and looking at the progress of the battle under a rain of shrapnel, which I can only call fearful. It was Mr Churchill, who had come to view the situation himself. It must be confessed that it is not easy to find in the whole of Europe a Minister who would be capable of smoking peacefully under that shellfire. He smiled, and looked quite satisfied.

'Courage is rightly esteemed the first of human qualities . . . because it is the quality which guarantees all others.' When he met a young officer whose colleagues were praising him for an act of bravery, but

who was too modest to say what he had done, Churchill told him: *'Young man, do not be ashamed of courage.'*

Churchill was anxious to acknowledge that *'The part of the army that really counts for ending the war is this killing, fighting, suffering part'* – the soldiers at the front – and felt that whatever the problems, they should receive all the support possible. When a colleague of his, Major Morton, returned from seeing the artillery commander to say, 'I'm afraid, Colonel, there is no way in which you can have the barrage you want. The General says it cannot be done,' Churchill asked him what his own view was. 'I feel, sir, it should be done.' *'Well, Major,'* came the reply, *'answer me this: What are generals but promoted majors?'*

His time in the trenches was enough to reignite his former spirit, and he was soon sure he was the person to sort out the war, writing to Clementine in February 1916, *'There is a great lack of "drive" throughout the administration of the army . . . This war is one of mechanics and brains, and mere sacrifice of brave and devoted infantry is no substitute and never will be. By God I would make them skip if I had the power – even for a month.'* He resigned his commission and returned home in early May.

He had to wait over a year more to return to the government. In July 1917 the new Prime Minister, his old friend, David Lloyd George, offered him the post of Minister for Munitions. In the meantime an inquiry into the Gallipoli Campaign was carried out by the Dardanelles Commission. Churchill thought his actions would be vindicated; he believed – with hindsight – that if the Allied attack on the Dardanelles had been as he had envisaged it – a strong, united, combined military and naval attack – the course of the First World War might have been quite different and much shorter. *'History will vindicate the conception, and the errors and execution will, on the whole, leave me clear,'* he wrote to his brother Jack. *'My one fatal mistake was trying to achieve a great enterprise without having the plenary authority which could so easily have carried it to success.'* In his response to the draft Commission Report, he wrote, *'Contemporaries have condemned the men who tried to force the Dardanelles – History will condemn those who did not aid them.'*

The reaction of the *Morning Post* to Churchill's new appointment was blunt: 'We confidently anticipate that he will continue to make colossal blunders at the cost of the nation.' It also remarked that the appointment proved that 'although we have not yet invented the unsinkable ship, we have discovered the unsinkable politician,' inadvertently putting a finger on one of the characteristics that were to contribute to Churchill's greatness and to deflect a disastrous outcome to the next war.

It is worth noting that, perhaps as a result of his months at the Western Front, Churchill seems to have become more aware of the contribution made by ordinary people. In a speech to the House of Commons in April 1918 – his words a foretaste of the speeches that sustained the Allies through the Second World War – he said:

> *No demand is too novel or too sudden to be met. No need is too unexpected to be supplied. No strain is too prolonged for the patience of our people. No suffering nor peril daunts their hearts. Instead of quarrelling, giving way as we do from time to time to moods of*

*pessimism and irritation, we ought to be thankful that if
such trials and dangers were destined for our country
we are here to share them, and to see them slowly and
surely overcome.*

Like his 1914 declaration *'The maxim of the British
people is "Business as usual"'*, such words have political
advantage in that they appeal to people's self-worth.

Also characteristic of Churchill was magnanimity in
victory. As it became clear by the summer of 1918 that
the Allies were winning, he declared, *'We are not asking
for the unconditional surrender of the German nation
. . . We do not seek to ruin Germany.'*

(Magnanimity was also characteristic of his personal
life. There exist a number of accounts from people who
angered him through their mistakes or stupidity who,
after they'd been admonished, were forgiven. Even,
according to Detective Inspector Thompson, the car
driver who knocked down and nearly killed Churchill on
a New York street was forgiven, though in fact Churchill
was quick to say it had been entirely his fault: he'd been
looking the wrong way as he crossed the road, unused to
American traffic. The driver was an unemployed Italian
truck driver, who, appalled by the accident, called at the
hospital every day for the week or so that Churchill was
there. Clementine, hearing that he was unemployed,
tried to give him a cheque but it was politely declined.
After Clementine, the young man was the first to visit
Churchill when he was well enough to receive visitors,
and left with a signed copy of Churchill's latest book, *The
Unknown War* – the US edition of *The Eastern Front*.)
Professor Lindemann sent Churchill a telegram inform-
ing him that the impact of the vehicle was equal to 6,000

foot-pounds of energy and that his body had been moved with a strength of 8,000 horse-power, intelligence which doubtless helped speed up his friend's recovery.

As Churchill would later remark in 1920, *'Politics are almost as exciting as war, and quite as dangerous. In war you can only be killed once, but in politics many times.'* In mid-1917, recovering from his political death, he set about his work as Minister for Munitions with vigour and enthusiasm. He did all he could to ensure that the Allies had what they needed in the way of guns, shells and aeroplanes – and the tanks, upon which he had been working tirelessly to develop and deploy. In 1918, the Royal Air Force had been formed by amalgamating the Royal Flying Corps with the Royal Naval Air Service, and was by now the world's largest air force. Thanks to Churchill's initial enthusiasm, over the next twenty years the RAF was developed as a strategic bombing force; by the late 1930s a fleet of monoplane bombers had been formed, to which were added fast, well-armed interceptor aircraft for defence against enemy bombers.

In October 1919, a Royal Commission reported that 'it was primarily due to the receptivity, courage and driving force of the Rt Hon. Winston Spencer Churchill that the general idea of the use of such an instrument of warfare as the Tank was converted into practical shape'. In his honour one of the British tank designs deployed in the Second World War was named after him . . . though from his speech to the Commons in July 1942, it was a bit of a double-edged compliment: *'It had many defects and teething troubles, and when these became apparent the tank was appropriately rechristened the "Churchill".'* (The tank in question, which had been in use for a couple of years or so, had good qualities – it was relatively roomy and virtually unstoppable – but, unlike Churchill, was undergunned and rather slow.)

Churchill was, comparatively speaking, politically more subdued for some years to come, although there were some remarks about his interference. Field Marshal Haig, C-in-C of the British forces in France, for instance, had 'no doubt that Winston means to do his utmost to provide the army with all it requires, but at the same time he can hardly help meddling in the larger questions of strategy and tactics; for the solution of the latter he has no real training, and his agile mind only makes him a danger because he can persuade Lloyd George to adopt and carry out the most idiotic policy.' And in November 1921, by which time Churchill was Colonial Secretary, Lord Curzon wrote to him crossly, 'I often wonder what would be your attitude if in the administration of your department you were subject to the constant interference of a colleague from which I have to suffer.'

With the end of the war, the eternal question of Ireland rose again. (It was said that he once remarked, *We have always found the Irish a bit odd. They refuse to be English.*' There is a suggestion of admiration in the words; something of a rebel – or individualist – himself, such a trait would have struck a sympathetic chord in him.)

The newly named Irish Republican Army, led by Michael Collins, began to use force, to counter which Churchill raised, in 1919, a Special Division of the Royal Ulster Constabulary largely drawn from unemployed veterans of the Great War. Commonly known as the Black and Tans, from their dark green and khaki uniform, they gained a reputation for brutality, which merely exacerbated the violence of the IRA. By this time, Churchill, now Secretary of State for the Colonies, was working for peace: '*It is of great public importance to get a respite in Ireland . . .*' he told the Commons in May 1921. The violence carried on until that summer, when an uneasy truce was called, leading to the Irish Treaty of December 1921.

Churchill described a meeting with Michael Collins in *The World Crisis*, volume IV: *The Aftermath*:

> '*You hunted me night and day!*' he exclaimed. '*You put a price on my head!*'
>
> 'Wait a minute,' *I said*. 'You are not the only one!' *And I took from my wall the framed copy of the reward offered for my recapture from the Boers*. 'At any rate, yours was a good price – £5,000. Look at me – £25 dead or alive. How would you like that?' *He read the paper, and as he took it in he broke into a hearty laugh.*

Collins, who was shot dead less than a year later, was to say, 'Tell Winston we could never have done without him.'

Many Irish, however, did not share this view, never forgetting the early threats of force, and the Black and Tans, and seeing Churchill as a near-villain. One of Churchill's bodyguards, Edmund Murray, told the story of how, years later, after the Second World War, Churchill's plane, on the way to the States, landed at Shannon to refuel before crossing the Atlantic. There Murray went to order some duty-free Irish whiskey for his Secret Service friends in the States. The Irishman at the counter said he'd have a box ready for him to pick up, and asked what name he should put on it. 'Murray,' he was told.

When Murray arrived to pick up his box, the man handed it to him, and asked, 'Can ye tell me, Mr Murray, what's a man with a name like Murray doing working for an old bastard like Churchill?'

Back on the aircraft, Murray told this to Churchill, who roared with laughter and then related the story to his wife. She was silent, then, after about five minutes piped, 'But he was wrong, Winston, he was quite wrong – you *do* know who your father was!'

With post-war anti-climax – Lloyd George's promised 'fit land for heroes to live in' never materialized – and economic recession, the government was rapidly losing support. Russia's revolution worried Churchill more than it did his colleagues – *'There is not one single social or economic principle or concept in the philosophy of the Russian Bolshevik which has not been realized, carried into action, and enshrined in immutable laws a million years ago by the white ant,'* he was to remark – and he could not persuade them to support the White Russians, while relations with Turkey were far from happy. Churchill busied himself in the Middle East, where he aroused some controversy.

After the Great War, Mesopotamia (Iraq) was occupied by the British Army, Britain having been granted a mandate to control the area. As Minister for War and Air, Churchill estimated that around 25,000 British and 80,000 Indian troops would be needed to keep control – with air power, he argued, these numbers could be cut down to 4,000 and 10,000, respectively. He won the government over, and when, in 1920, there was an uprising of more than 100,000 armed Arab and Kurdish tribesmen, the RAF was sent in, dropping over the next few months 97 tons of bombs and killing 9,000 Irāqis. This failed to end the resistance, which continued to pose a threat to British rule. Churchill advocated *'the provision of some kind of asphyxiating bombs calculated to cause disablement of some kind but not death . . . for use in preliminary operations against turbulent tribes'*; also saying *'I am strongly in favour of using poisoned gas against uncivilized tribes to spread a lively terror'*. This unwarranted lack of humanity is disappointing in one destined to be considered 'the greatest', and remains unforgiven in the Middle East and elsewhere, yet it is perhaps consistent with his paternalistic, white-supremacist Victorian upbringing, which had taught him that the British Empire was the greatest and that, while Britain had a duty to rule her colonies well, her colonies should be grateful to her for civilizing them; those who rebelled were not *'civilized'* – they came somewhere above the animal kingdom but below the white man and those 'natives' who had been civilized – and should be dealt with firmly. He insisted that the weapons would cause *'only discomfort or illness, but not death'*. Regrettably, he was mistaken. (This apparent callousness reappears in notes he made for a speech delivered in private session in June 1940, during the Battle of Britain, referring to being bombed: *'Learn to get used to it. Eels get used to skinning.'* It is most likely, however, that he was looking for a striking metaphor with which to jolt his colleagues.)

From a personal viewpoint, 1921 was a bad year for Churchill. In April his brother-in-law, Bill Hozier, committed suicide; in June, Churchill's mother died as a result of a fall; her death was followed, two months later by that of Thomas Walden, a *'faithful retainer'*; and then his three-year-old daughter Marigold died, possibly of diphtheria, a now easily treated disease. Of the many letters Churchill received, one from his old friend Lord Grey, stood out:

> You were saying the other day how closely death had pressed home to you this year: and now it has come again in a particularly poignant form. The death of a little child seems to me to be more difficult than any other to reconcile with any scheme we can imagine of the fitness and purpose of things. But I know you are brave enough to bear suffering and I think you are strong enough to enlarge your outlook and to grow and not to be withered by anything you have to go through. It may be harder still for your wife, who has not your work to pass the time for her.

In a letter to Clementine some eight months later, Churchill referred to their child's death as *'a gaping wound, whenever one touches it and removes the bandages and plasters of daily life'.*

In October 1922, Churchill fell ill with appendicitis, the Conservatives left the coalition government and Lloyd George resigned his premiership. As a result of having to have his appendix out (and surgery was in those days cruder, recovery times longer than today), Churchill missed much of the campaigning, and when he managed to make it from his sick-bed, *'I was struck by looks of passionate hatred on the faces of some of the younger men and women. Indeed but for my helpless condition I am sure they would have attacked me,'* he wrote in *Thoughts and Adventures* (1932). Come the end of the electoral campaign he was *'without an office, without a seat, without a party, and without an appendix'.*

Chapter 5

The Brilliant
Wayward Child

COMMENTATORS DO NOT TIRE of pointing out that had Churchill died in the Great War or at any time during the twenty years that followed, he would be remembered only as a turbulent politician, who upset many and caused trouble. Certainly not as a 'great man' or 'great Briton' (though possibly as a 'great nuisance'). There is in what his colleagues had to say about him a recurring picture that recalls the little boy jumping around the classroom table, annoying everyone with his exhibitionism and quarrelsome behaviour; or the dashing cavalry officer galloping into the fray; or the cloaked figure directing the traffic in panic-stricken Antwerp – and the compulsive interferer. Yet many of the remarks and complaints about Churchill also acknowledge his untiring work, his 'genius', and often reveal a fondness for him. Charles Hobhouse wrote in his diary for 17 July 1912, 'Churchill was most abusive and insulting . . . He is really a spoilt child endowed by some chance with the brain of a genius.' 'He is intolerable! Noisy, longwinded and full of perorations,' protested Asquith in 1915.

In March 1916, when Churchill was on leave from the front and made a speech in Parliament outlining unpopular suggestions for the Admiralty, Admiral Sir Hedworth Meux commented, 'The hon. and gallant Member is a very old friend of mine, and I have received many kindnesses from him, but there are limits to endurance . . . We all wish him a great deal of success in France, and we hope that he will stay there.'

Field Marshal Sir Henry Wilson (who was to be assassinated in 1922 over the issue of Irish Home Rule) said of him, 'His judgement is always at fault, and he is hopeless when in power.' He also acknowledged, however, Churchill's 'many good qualities'.

Margot Asquith, second wife of the wartime Prime Minister, is said to have claimed that 'He would kill his own mother just so that he could use her skin to make a drum to beat his own praises.' She also called him, in a letter to Balfour in 1916 – at a time when tempers were running high following a dramatic and ill-considered speech by Churchill in which he systematically demolished the Admiralty he had recently had to leave – 'a hound of the lowest sense of political honour, a fool of the lowest judgement & contemptible. He cured me of oratory in the House & bored me with oratory in the Home!'

In June 1922, the Assistant Secretary to the Cabinet, Thomas Jones, recorded in his diary that the Prime Minister (David Lloyd George) had 'compared Winston to a chauffeur who apparently is perfectly sane and drives with great skill for months, then suddenly he takes you over a precipice'. A couple of years later, when Baldwin was considering whether or not to offer Churchill a Cabinet position, Jones commented, 'I would certainly have him inside, not out. He is incapable of being permanently loyal to anybody but Winston, and you must count on your loyal men to withstand him.'

The *Morning Post* in its outraged reaction to Churchill's appointment as Minister of Munitions in 1917 seethed about the 'unsinkable politician . . . whose overwhelming conceit led him to imagine he was Nelson at sea and a Napoleon on land'. When Baldwin was Prime Minister he put Churchill on the Coal Committee trying to deal with unrest among miners, and another Committee member observed that Churchill was 'jolly difficult when he's in a Napoleonesque attitude, dictating instructions in military metaphors, and the spotlight full on him . . . he is a most brilliant fellow, but his gifts aren't those of judgement, nor of appreciating industry, nor of a negotiator.'

Some time later, when he was Chancellor in 1926, Churchill was given the editorship of a government newspaper set up for the duration of the General Strike, the *British Gazette*, to 'keep him busy and stop him doing worse things'. He soon put people's backs up – 'He thinks he is Napoleon, but curiously enough the men who have been printing all their life in the various processes happen to know more about their job than he does,' complained John Colin Campbell Davidson, Financial and Parliamentary Secretary to the Admiralty, who was also on the paper's editorial board. Churchill's *'foul-weather friend'*, Lord Beaverbrook, the newspaper proprietor, remarked, 'Churchill on top of the wave has in him the stuff of which tyrants are made.'

Clement Attlee, Labour Prime Minister after the Second World War (and Churchill's deputy during it), was to say, 'Fifty per cent of Winston is genius, fifty per cent bloody fool. He *will* behave like a child.' The Labour politician, Aneurin 'Nye' Bevan did not acknowledge the genius part – at various times he was to call Churchill 'a man suffering from petrified adolescence', a 'bloated bladder of lies' and someone who 'never spares himself in conversation. He gives himself so generously that hardly anybody else is permitted to give anything in his presence'.

So he would have been remembered as more than just a troublemaker – at times childish, noisy, rude, impetuous, full of himself, an exhibitionist, certainly; but also industrious, warm, kind, with a busy mind ('Churchill has a hundred ideas a day, of which four are good ideas,' President Roosevelt is reported to have said) and – even – a genius.

Then, there were the books – he published over forty, most of them histories, highly readable and usually written from a personal standpoint (Attlee suggested that his *History of the English-Speaking Peoples* could be given the alternative title of *Things in History that Interested Me*). Altogether, he published more words than Charles Dickens and Walter Scott together. And they were certainly not forgettable like this fine passage from *The World Crisis*:

> *The British offensive against Passchendaele unrolled its sombre fate. The terrific artillery pulverized the ground, smashing simultaneously the German trenches and the ordinary drainage. By sublime devotion and frightful losses, small indentations were made upon the German front. In six weeks at the farthest point we had advanced four miles. Soon the rain descended, and the vast crater*

> fields became a choking fetid mud in which men,
> animals and tanks floundered and perished hopelessly.

By the early 1920s, Churchill had produced some twelve books, including collections of speeches. In 1923 he published the first of his five-volume account of the First World War, *The World Crisis* (1923–31), to which was added a sixth volume, *The Eastern Front*. In a speech in 1986, Sir Anthony Montague Browne recalled Churchill's Cabinet colleague Sir Samuel Hoare announcing, 'Winston has written a huge book all about himself and called it *The World Crisis*.' Churchill rejoined: '*I have not always been wrong. History will bear me out, particularly as I shall write that history myself.*'

Balfour wrote to a friend: 'I am immersed in Winston's brilliant autobiography, disguised as a history of the universe.'

The *Observer*'s J. L. Garvin, calling *The World Crisis* 'a whale among minnows', commented that 'Mr Churchill, when they attack him, defends himself. He does it with such an amplitude of evidence, and a panoply of proof and a general effect so wicked that his habitual accusers must regard his book as not only a misdemeanour, but an outrage . . . Much the best of all war books on the British side.'

In the States, the work was equally well received. 'Winston wanted to be a war wizard, and there he failed, but in the wizardry of words he is triumphant,' said *The New York Times*:

Over his own vicissitudes he casts the spell . . . it is the spell of a calculated – sometimes an artificial –

detachment . . . He makes no excuses . . . He avoids the querulous, the malicious, the jealous note . . . He does not pretend to have been consistent. Good, bad or indifferent, he gives his reasons for whatever was done or left undone. The reasons are those noted at the time . . . there is no wisdom after the event. It is clever. It is masterful. But it is also Churchill . . . Churchill is too interesting for real sagacity.

Baldwin was more succinct, as well as pointed: 'If I could write as you do, I should never bother about making speeches.'

During the first half of the 1920s the country jolted uncomfortably from Prime Minister to Prime Minister. Andrew Bonar Law took the premiership on Lloyd George's resignation in 1922, but he became seriously ill and resigned within months, dying soon after. Stanley Baldwin took his place as leader of the Conservatives and was Prime Minister briefly in 1923; another election, and, with Liberal support, Labour came into power in January 1924, with Ramsay MacDonald as the first Labour Prime Minister. This government lasted less than ten months.

Churchill lost elections in 1923 and 1924; disappointed in his Liberal colleagues' support for Labour (or, could it be, lack of support for himself?), he decided to cast his lot in with the Conservative Party, and in September, he accepted an offer from the Conservative Party's Constituency Committee in Epping (later Woodford) to stand for Parliament next time an election was held as a 'Constitutionalist' with Conservative Party support.

There was growing unease about the Labour government's friendly relations with Soviet Russia and in October Parliament was dissolved and a general election held – Churchill had a considerable majority, and remained the constituency's MP for the next forty years.

In 1920 he had said of a fellow Liberal MP who had crossed the floor to join the ailing Socialist Party: *'It is the only time I've ever seen a rat swimming towards a sinking ship.'* Now, in 1924, he himself had crossed the floor – and for a second time. He claimed, somewhat disingenuously, *'I am what I have always been – a Tory Democrat. Force of circumstance has compelled me to serve with another party, but my views have never changed, and I should be glad to give effect to them by rejoining the Conservatives!'* As he remarked, not a little smugly, *'Anyone can rat, but it takes a certain amount of ingenuity to re-rat.'*

As Chancellor, a couple of years later, he was accused in the Commons by his Labour predecessor at the Treasury, Philip Snowden, of switching positions on his budget. Churchill pointed out that there was nothing wrong with change if it was in the right direction, to which Snowden countered that 'The Honourable gentleman is an authority on that.'

Churchill retorted gleefully: *'To improve is to change; to be perfect is to change often.'*

Many years later, an old man, he was recalling his early life in conversation with Anthony Montague Browne (which included the surprising revelation that as a boy his ambition had been to play the cello) and mentioned how, when in his teens, he had considered going into the Church. *'I wonder what would have become of me then?'* he mused. He was not terribly amused when his Private Secretary suggested he would have crossed the floor and become Pope.

When the Conservative Party won the 1924 general election, to Churchill's surprised delight, the new Prime Minister, Stanley Baldwin, invited him to be Chancellor of the Exchequer.

'This fulfils my ambition,' he told Baldwin. *'I still have my father's robe as Chancellor. I shall be proud to serve you in this splendid office.'* He also remarked, *'You have done more for me than Lloyd George ever did.'* (Whether it was at this time or at a later date is not clear, but Churchill's grandson tells a story of Lloyd George, in the days before they had telephones in the offices of the House of Commons, sticking his head out of a phone booth and, seeing Churchill walking by, calling to him and asking if he would lend him sixpence so that he could telephone a friend . . . 'My grandfather, making a great demonstration of digging deep into his pocket to produce a coin, and with a mischievous grin on his face, replies: *"Here is a shilling – now you can call* all *your friends!"'*)

The *Manchester Guardian* greeted the news of the new Chancellor sourly: 'Mr Churchill for the second time has – shall we say – quitted the sinking ship, and for the second time the reward of this fine instinct has been not safety only but high promotion.'

Austen Chamberlain, the new Foreign Secretary and half-brother of Neville Chamberlain, wrote to express his concern to Baldwin. 'I am alarmed at the news that you have made Winston Chancellor, not because I do not wish Winston well but because I fear that this particular appointment will be a great shock to the Party.' He was to be disappointed by the new Chancellor's lack of support for his Locarno Treaties, designed to strengthen security in Europe.

In 1909, when he was President of the Board of Trade, Churchill had supported the Chancellor of the Exchequer, David Lloyd George, in restricting expenditure on the Navy; the moment he became First Lord of the Admiralty, in 1911, he agitated to increase spending on the Navy. Now, as Chancellor of the Exchequer, he again reversed his stance, and became rather less keen on spending on defence. A contemporary cartoon in *Punch* showed Churchill with a gun, patrolling the 'Exchequer Woods'; the caption read 'Poacher into Gamekeeper'.

He began 1925 with his first budget, in which he proposed to reduce income tax – and keep defence expenditure to the minimum. Admiral Sir David Beatty (the man who had told Churchill that from afar the Omdurman cavalry charge had reminded him of plum duff) now First Sea Lord, was far from pleased. 'That extraordinary fellow Winston has gone mad,' he spluttered in a letter of 26 January to his wife. 'Economically mad, and no sacrifice is too great to achieve . . . 1/- off the Income Tax this Budget . . . ' In the event the one-shilling tax cut was reduced to sixpence. It was now four shillings in the pound, or 20 per cent. Churchill also introduced schemes for widows' and orphans' pensions (an emotive issue in the aftermath of the Great War), and for reforming the payment of old-age pensions.

John Davidson, who as Financial and Parliamentary Secretary to the Admiralty was also displeased, put his finger on why Churchill changed his outlook on expenditure when he later wrote:

> It was characteristic of Winston Churchill that he put the whole of his energy into what he believed to be the right policy of the Department over which he presided. When he was at the Exchequer he believed that he was the keeper of the public purse and must keep a most severe control over all spending departments. And, although an old First Lord of the Admiralty, he felt compelled to oppose the expenditure regarded as the minimum required by the Navy . . . This led to a first-class row.

Unfortunately for Beatty, Churchill was familiar enough with the job of First Sea Lord to send him in February a long list of cost-cutting suggestions, adding, *'It is no good telling me the First Sea Lord cannot do this if he lets it be known that it is his wish. Even when First Lord, as you know, I often found this amount and larger amounts in a few mornings with a blue pencil.'*

In a letter to his wife, Beatty said wearily, 'I have to tackle Winston . . . It takes a good deal out of me when dealing with a man of his calibre with a very quick brain. A false step, remark, or even gesture is immediately fastened upon, so I have to keep my wits about me.'

Churchill's mistake – which he was not allowed to forget – was to decide to do something he did not initially want to do. This was to return Britain to the Gold Standard, at the pre-war rate, which, as it turned out, seriously overvalued the pound. Before the First World War most countries were on the Gold Standard, by which the value of a currency was defined in terms of gold, for which the currency could be exchanged, originally established to facilitate developing international trade. During the Great War, the system fell by the wayside, but in Britain a number of financial experts, including the Governor of the Bank of England and very senior officials of the Treasury, called for a 'Return to Gold' (a rallying cry not unlike the call 'Back to Basics'), insisting that it would be the best route to take for the country. Churchill, bolstered by an article by John Maynard Keynes, and with the support of the Chairman of Barclay's, Reginald McKenna (with whom he had exchanged jobs in 1911, when Home Secretary became First Lord and vice versa, and who had been Liberal Chancellor in 1915–16), resisted returning Britain to the Gold Standard to begin with. *'The Treasury has never, it seems to me, faced the profound significance of what Mr Keynes calls "The paradox of unemployment amidst dearth",'* he wrote to Sir Otto Niemeyer at the Treasury. *'The Governor shows himself perfectly happy in the spectacle of Britain possessing the finest credit in the world simultaneously with a million and a quarter unemployed.'* The pro-Gold Standard faction accused him of having his 'spiritual home in the Keynes-McKenna sanctuary'.

'If we are to take the very important step of removing the embargo on gold export, it is essential that we should be prepared to answer any criticism which may be subsequently made upon our policy,' Churchill wrote to Montague Norman, the Governor of the Bank of England. Eventually, he invited both sides to dinner to discuss the matter. The pros won the day, with McKenna giving in to their argument that inflation was a greater danger to the country than the deflation and growing unemployment predicted by Keynes. Churchill bowed to apparently superior knowledge. When he

made his Budget speech, no party criticized the decision. Keynes wrote a book whose title alone was enough to pin all blame on Churchill: *The Economic Consequences of Mr Churchill*. Keynes was, of course, right in his predictions, albeit a bit harsh in his attack on Churchill – although Churchill recognized that, as Chancellor, he was ultimately responsible for the decision. As he once said, '*The price of greatness is responsibility*' – but he wasn't great yet.

At the time, his speech was an overwhelming success. 'One of the most striking Budget speeches of recent years,' according to Baldwin, who wrote to the King that it

> was a first-rate example of Mr Churchill's characteristic style. At one moment he would be expounding quietly and lucidly facts and figures relating to the financial position during the past and current years. At another moment, inspired and animated by the old political controversies on the subject of tariff reform, he indulged in witty levity and humour, which come as a refreshing relief in the dry atmosphere of a Budget speech. At another moment . . . he soared into emotional flights of rhetoric in which he has few equals; and throughout the speech he showed that he is not only possessed of consummate ability as a parliamentarian, but also all the versatility of an actor.

In a speech he gave in the autumn of 1925, Churchill alluded to his more popular measures: '*In that Budget I committed some serious crimes. I reduced the income tax, and I differentiated the income tax in favour of the smaller income-tax payer . . . I have been scolded for these evil deeds.*'

He was happy as his Finance Bill made its way

through the House. '*I am driving forward at least ten large questions, and many smaller ones all inter-related and centring on the Budget,*' he wrote to Clementine in June. '*So far I am getting my own way in nearly everything. But it is a most laborious business, so many stages having to be gone through, so many people having to be consulted, and so much detail having to be mastered or explored in one way or another.*'

Neville Chamberlain, then Minister for Health, was approving. He wrote to Baldwin in August 1925,

> Looking back over our first session I think our Chancellor has done very well, all the better because he hasn't been what he was expected to be. He hasn't dominated the Cabinet, though undoubtedly he has influenced it . . . He hasn't intrigued for the leadership, but he has been a tower of debating strength in the House of Commons . . . What a brilliant creature he is! I like him. I like his humour and vitality, I like his courage . . . Mercurial! A much abused word, but it is the literal description of his temperament.

That was before the effects of the return to the Gold Standard began to show themselves. Three years later, Chamberlain was not so sure: 'There is too deep a difference between our natures for me to feel at home with him or to regard him with affection. He is a brilliant wayward child who compels admiration but who wears out his guardians with the constant strain he puts on them.'

In August 1925, in an article published in *Atlantic Monthly*, the writer and journalist Ian Colvin expressed some of the doubts held by some of Churchill's colleagues:

We shall see. There are, on the other hand, a good many
Conservatives – including some of the staunchest and
least self-seeking – who are disappointed and almost
estranged by this appointment. They allege that Mr
Churchill has made at least one capital blunder in every
one of the many offices he has held; that – what is worse
– he has never shown any sign of political principle; and
that his only consistency has been in the pursuit of his
own political fortunes. They argue that the leopard does
not change his spots nor the Ethiopian his skin, and they
fear that even the brilliancy of the new Chancellor is
erratic and may lead to some far-shining and illustrious
calamity.

The consequences of Britain's return to the Gold
Standard were as the doubters had foreseen. With the
pound at its high pre-war exchange rate, British goods
were too expensive and could not compete with those of
other countries, and prices had to come down.
Economic disaster led to unemployment and a crisis in
the coal industry, with the pit owners reducing wages
(offering the alternative of longer hours for unreduced
pay) and the miners going on strike. Years later, in 1945,
the Labour Prime Minister Clement Attlee rounded on
Churchill, calling him the 'most disastrous Chancellor of
the century' for putting Britain back on the Gold
Standard – then conceding, 'He sinned, no doubt in all
ignorance, but much of our troubles today can be traced
back to that error of ignorance and his simple trust of
others in a field where he had little knowledge.'

Had the miners' strike not led to the General Strike
and attempts from the trade unions to bring down the
government, matters would have followed a quite

different path. The threat of a general strike was clear by the end of 1925, as was the fact that there were those in the unions who wanted to bring about a general election and vote in a Socialist government that would, among other things, nationalize the coal industry. *'The inherent vice of capitalism is the unequal sharing of blessings; the inherent vice of socialism is the equal sharing of miseries,'* Churchill is said to have observed. This leaves one to wonder what he believed was the answer – perhaps it lay in his own philosophy: *'The essential principle is personal freedom, the right of the individual to make the best of himself, or, within limits, the worst of himself, if he chooses; the stimulation of all these individual activities by the reward of enterprise, toil, and thrift; and their reconciliation through the laws.'*

Churchill is also supposed to have said: *'It is a socialist idea that making profits is a vice; I consider the real vice is making losses.'* In a speech in November 1925, striking an exaggerated note of warning about the threatened general strike, he said, *'The Socialist in his folly, and the Communist in his malice, would undermine and fatally wreck the pillars of our national prosperity . . . the Communist thinks he can smash his way through by violence, and the Socialist believes he can do it by humbug . . .'*

He was at first sympathetic towards the miners (as well as anxious to avert a general strike) and did his utmost to get a good settlement for them. Maurice Ashley, who later worked for Churchill, said, many years later, that

> the name of Churchill was anathema to me because we young socialists believed that Churchill was chiefly

responsible for crushing the General Strike of 1926, called on behalf of the coal miners. As a matter of fact, as we now know, Churchill was sympathetic to the claims of the miners, who were then paid a pitiful wage, and he did not care for the coal-owners. He would have liked minimum wages to be guaranteed to the miners and a limitation imposed on the profits of the owners, but he was overruled by the Prime Minister, Stanley Baldwin.

So it was all Baldwin's fault – but Ashley had by then fallen under his employer's spell . . . Thomas Jones observed in September 1926, that Churchill 'was quite prepared to go to great lengths in the way of legislation on hours, wages and conditions', but once other unions had come out in support of the miners in May, it became for Churchill another battle – unions against government: *'Either the country will break the General Strike, or the General Strike will break the country,'* he wrote, characteristically throwing himself into the fray. One weapon he used was the government paper, the *British Gazette*, in which the language he used was often unacceptably intemperate. 'After a great fight,' recorded John Davidson, 'Winston agreed to be blue-pencilled, and from that moment my blue pencil was seldom idle.'

In the event, the General Strike lasted not much longer than a week, and the miners' strike petered out over the following months. But it left a sour taste.

The failure of the General Strike saw Churchill return to form. A few months after the strike had ended, during a debate in the Commons, a Labour Member intimated the possibility of renewed industrial action against planned legislation against unions. Churchill stood up: *'I have no wish to make threats which would disturb the House and cause bad blood,'* he began in the tones of a headmaster promising dire punishment. He paused before continuing *'. . . But this I must say. Make your minds perfectly clear that if ever you let loose upon us a General Strike, we will let loose upon you . . .'* A loaded silence followed, while the Members stirred uncomfortably and prepared themselves for an acrimonious session, *'. . . another* British Gazette.*'*

He brought the House down and successfully deflected any further aggravation.

Churchill as Chancellor was no more disastrous than most. He made mistakes, but also formulated some workable budgets. He is criticized mainly for taking bad advice over the Gold Standard, which was ruinous for Britain's economy, and led to the General Strike, which in turn did nothing to help repair Britain's economy. He cut defence spending – but at the time there was no obvious aggression from other nations. Europe seemed more or less peaceful and the Soviet Union was sufficiently distant not to pose too great a threat. The Admiralty warned that Japan, far away in the Pacific, was flexing its muscles. *'A war with Japan!'* he wrote to Baldwin. *'But why should there be a war with Japan? I do not believe there is the slightest chance of it in our lifetime.'* As he once remarked, a politician needed to have *'The ability to foretell what is going to happen tomorrow, next week, next month, and next year. And to have the ability afterwards to explain why it didn't happen.'* (By 1943 he had realized that it is better not to try to foretell the future: *'I always avoid prophesying beforehand, because it is much better policy to prophesy after the event has already taken place.'*)

Churchill worked hard, though Samuel Hoare, Secretary of State for Air since 1922, contemplating Churchill's second Budget plans, was apprehensive, saying that the Chancellor was convinced 'that he is to be the prophet to lead us into the Promised Land in which there will be no income tax and everyone will live happily ever afterwards. The trouble is that he has got so many schemes tumbling over each other in his mind, that I am beginning to wonder whether he will be able to pull any one of them out of the heap.'

His third budget speech in 1927, which introduced all that *'could be done by way of taxation without checking a trade revival'*, was well received by the Prime Minister at least. In a letter to the King, Baldwin wrote, 'Mr Churchill as a star turn has a power of attraction which nobody in the House of Commons can excel . . . There is in Mr Churchill an undercurrent of buoyant mischievousness which frequently makes its appearance on the surface in some picturesque phrase or playful sally at the expense of his opponents.' Lord Winterton was equally impressed, writing to a friend, 'I thought it a masterpiece, and about the best I have ever heard. Winston is a wonderful fellow . . . head and shoulders above anyone else in the House (not excluding Lloyd George) in Parliamentary position, and both oratorical and debating skill . . . he has suddenly acquired, quite late in his Parliamentary life, an immense fund of tact, patience, good humour and banter on almost all occasions.'

Churchill's fourth budget presented a scheme to revive British industry by removing industrial rates, and was well received; as was his fifth, in 1929, which was introduced in what the *Sunday Times* described as 'the most brilliantly entertaining of modern Budget speeches', while Neville Chamberlain wrote in his diary that it 'was one of the best he has made, and kept the House fascinated by its wit, audacity, adroitness and power'.

Perhaps it is because the Prime Minister and other Members enjoyed Churchill's speeches so much that he remained at the Treasury for an unusually long time. For what seems to stand out in Churchill's stint as Chancellor is not so much his success or even lack of success at the Treasury as his entertainment value. It was not enough, however, to gain the Conservative Party another term in government, and at the next general election, a few months later, the Conservatives were defeated by the Labour Party, and Ramsay MacDonald began his second term as Prime Minister.

Chapter 6

Books, Arms
and the King

'THERE WAS NO INTERVIEW. Churchill sat by me on a sofa and said, "*I hear you are going to work for me.*" Lindemann asked Churchill if he would like champagne for his lunch. Churchill replied, "*I always have beer for lunch.*"' Churchill needed someone to help him with his biography of his ancestor, the first Duke of Marlborough. Maurice Ashley was a clever young historian just graduated from Oxford and in need of a job, and a meeting at Lindemann's flat had been arranged. As an ardent socialist, however, he was not too keen on the idea of working for Churchill, whose name was 'anathema' to him. But he does not appear to have been given any choice. He was, on the spot, invited – or summoned – to Chartwell, the country house in Kent that the Churchills had bought seven years earlier, in 1922.

Churchill was a considerate and generous host; there was nothing he enjoyed more than having guests at his table, especially if he was the centre of attention. An eighteen-year-old friend of Randolph's described having dinner there one evening in 1929:

> We remained this evening at the round table until after
> midnight. The tablecloth was removed. Mr Churchill
> spent a blissful two hours demonstrating with the
> decanters and wine glasses how the Battle of Jutland
> was fought. He got worked up like a schoolboy, making
> barking noises in imitation of gun fire, and blowing
> smoke across the table in imitation of gun smoke.

Maurice Ashley does not mention any battles being
re-enacted on the dinner table, but he was certainly
generously plied with drink, and his apparent preference
never forgotten. 'Before dinner we had sherry, then
champagne, brandy and port. During the night I was
violently sick. On the following evening at dinner I
refused the port. *"Ah!"* said Churchill. *"I have some
excellent Madeira."* Afterwards, whenever I dined at
Chartwell, Churchill would say, *"Ashley likes Madeira."'*

'Winston was a meticulous host. He would watch
everyone all the time to see whether they wanted
anything,' Patrick Buchan-Hepburn told Churchill's
biographer Martin Gilbert.

> He was a tremendous gent in his own house. He was
> very quick to see anything that might hurt someone. He
> got very upset if someone told a story that might be
> embarrassing to somebody else in the room. He had a
> delicacy about other people's feelings. In his house and
> to his guests he was the perfection of thoughtfulness.

Without a ministerial post, now that the Labour
government was in power, Churchill had time to
concentrate on other things – his writing, for instance.
He had by now published about fifteen books, and was
earning well from them, but he needed to earn more

now that he only had an MP's salary to keep him, and his beloved Chartwell, in the manner to which he was accustomed. An assistant would help speed up his output.

Ever restless, however, he first made a trip to Canada and the United States (where, as related earlier, he ran up against the Prohibition), accompanied by his son Randolph, his brother Jack, and Jack's son Johnnie, who, like Randolph, was an undergraduate at Oxford. Clementine was unwell and had been advised not to travel; so she had to be content with letters and even – an exciting technical development – a telephone call from San Francisco. It is possible that Churchill felt that his son would derive some good from the journey – *'You appear to be leading a perfectly useless existence,'* he said to him, the words reminiscent of his father's words to him, though there the resemblance ended, for Churchill was much closer to his son than his father had been to him, and tempered criticism with kindness and affection.

Travelling on the same ship was fellow Conservative and Commons sparring partner Leo Amery, with whom Churchill argued about free trade and protection. 'He was very friendly about it,' Amery wrote in his diary, 'and only said that if I got my way he would retire from politics and devote himself to making money. He had been all that he wanted to be short of the highest post which he saw no prospect of, and anyhow politics were not what they had been.' This differs somewhat from another account of their shipboard arguments that relates that when Amery suggested that Churchill might find himself breaking away from the Conservative Party when it returned to tariffs and protectionism, he replied that *'I shall stick to you with all the loyalty of a leech.'*

*

Churchill's first encounter with Leo Amery had been many years before, when he had just started at Harrow. Within a few days of his arrival, he had come to appreciate the huge swimming pool and joined the other boys in pushing each other in. On one occasion he spotted a smallish boy standing near the edge with a towel round him. The temptation couldn't be resisted, and, thoughtfully hanging on to the towel, Winston gave the boy a good push into the water. This time, however, there was no laughter – the boy was furious and made for the side of the pool at speed. Before Winston knew what was happening he had been hurled into the pool. As he spluttered his way out, the other boys gathered round him full of dire promises as to what his fate would be: 'Do you know what you've done? It's Amery . . .' A sixth-former, an all-round champion sportsman, head of his house: retribution would be severe. Winston hastened to apologize: *'I am very sorry. I mistook you for a Fourth Form boy. You are so small.'* This was not terribly well received, so he added, *'My father, who is a great man, is also small.'* Young Amery was then gracious enough to accept his apology.

They went first to Canada, spending some days in Quebec. His son recalled how one evening, looking across the St Lawrence at the twinkling lights of the paper mills on the other side, Churchill, the occasional journalist, remarked sadly, *'Fancy cutting down all those beautiful trees we saw earlier today to make pulp for those bloody newspapers, and calling it civilization.'*

The Churchill party's tour of North America took in a great deal – they saw the Niagara Falls, visited the

Alberta oilfields; they went to San Francisco, Washington, DC, and New York; they were taken to Santa Catalina Island to fish for swordfish, and were shown round the Civil War battlefields, and much more besides, including the MGM Studios in Los Angeles and Hollywood.

Churchill was a great film fan, with a wide-ranging taste in what he watched – some would say lack of discrimination – but, as he once said to his son, then aged fifteen, when Randolph apologized to him for having dragged him from his work to see a 'trashy' film, *'We must lend ourselves to the illusion'*. On a sea voyage in 1941, for instance, he watched films starring Laurence Olivier and Vivien Leigh, Goofy and Donald Duck, Humphrey Bogart and Ida Lupino, and Laurel and Hardy . . . and a number of others. Sir Alexander Cadogan of the Foreign Office was on the same voyage. Some of the films he thought were 'awful bunk but the PM loves them and they keep him quiet'. Churchill found it relaxing to watch films late into the night after his very busy days, a habit he shared with Hitler and Stalin. The latter even sent him a film which he recommended highly, *Kutuzov*, about the retreat of Napoleon's armies from Moscow in 1812 – no doubt an allusion to the German armies who had similarly tried to invade Russia.

In 1928 Churchill wrote to Clementine that, *'I am becoming a film fan, and last week I went to see* The Last Command, *a very fine anti-Bolshevik film, and* Wings, *which is all about aeroplane fighting and perfectly marvellous.'* Some of his comments were less than critically incisive – after watching *Wuthering*

Heights, all he said was, '*What terrible weather they have in Yorkshire.*' He had a childish tendency to take films personally – thus he walked out of *Citizen Kane* (1941) because William Randolph Hearst, on whom the character Kane is based, was a friend of his; and in June 1940 Jock Colville noted, 'The PM went to a cinema to see the Dunkirk film and returned in rather a bad temper.' Churchill extended this to his pets – when watching the film of *Oliver Twist* at home he was careful to put a hand over his dog Rufus's eyes so that Rufus would not see Bill Sikes drown his dog. Years later, when he was an old man, Churchill continued to watch films avidly at home (he had projection equipment installed at Chequers in 1943, and at Chartwell in 1946). In 1962, his doctor, Dr Sneddon, recalled him watching *Sink the Bismarck*: 'He never took his eyes off it, and they lit up. He sat up and his usually pale face flushed. His cigar went out: he just held it; his mouth opened in rapt attention. Winston was fighting the battle over again.'

Once he became Prime Minster the problem of security made it impossible for Churchill to go out to cinemas; however, a friend of his, the Conservative MP Ronald Tree (like him, half American) had projection equipment at his home, Ditchley Park, a fine house north of Oxford, not far from Blenheim Palace. When, during the war, Chequers was considered too vulnerable to air attack (at least when there was moonlight) Churchill – having taken to Ditchley Park – decided to use the Trees' home as a weekend retreat, arriving with his entire entourage of secretaries and others, even guests. There, as well as attending to his business, and enjoying the Trees' hospitality, Churchill used to watch films. If he was staying at Blenheim he was sometimes driven there in a gig – Cyril Barfield, a groom at Ditchley Park, recollected that one evening as they were trotting along gently, Churchill grabbled the reins from him, growling, 'I'll *drive. At this rate the bloody butler will have locked the tantalus before I get there!'* Thereafter Cyril always drove Churchill at a more spirited pace to get him to the drinks cupboard in time.

When he visited Hollywood, Churchill met Charlie Chaplin, and in conversation with the comic actor, he asked what film part he would like to play next. Chaplin replied – and there was no sign that he was not utterly serious – 'I'd like to play Jesus Christ.'

Without batting an eyelid, WSC asked him, equally seriously, *'Have you cleared the rights?'*

One of the aims of this transatlantic trip had been to make money, of which he had high hopes. Speeches and articles and book deals paid for the tour, but even though he wrote to his wife, *'There are fortunes to be made in many directions'*, he did not make a fortune – he speculated and lost heavily with the Wall Street Crash, which happened to coincide with his visit to New York. Indeed, he dined with the great financier Bernard Baruch on Black Thursday, 29 October 1929. (He even claimed to have witnessed one of the famous suicides of ruined investors: *'Under my window, a gentleman cast himself down fifteen storeys, and was dashed to pieces.'*)

A further visit to the United States a couple of years later would, on the other hand, mark an upturn in his fortunes – although he did walk into the path of an oncoming car as he was crossing the road to Bernard Baruch's house, an accident in which he sustained severe bruising, a bad scalp wound and a couple of broken ribs, and which put him out of action for about three weeks. When he was in New York he stayed at the Plaza Hotel, and on the day that he was due to arrive there – so the story goes – the manager of the hotel, knowing nothing of Churchill's preferences in food and drink, and anxious to please him, telephoned the British Embassy in Washington. He was just explaining this to the person who answered the telephone when there was an interruption at the other end and a new voice came on the line: *'Yes?'*

'I am the director of the Plaza Hotel inquiring about Mr Churchill's tastes —'

'Mr Churchill,' the voice interrupted him, *'is a man of simple tastes – easily satisfied with the best.'*

The owner of the voice would have known, of course – it was Churchill himself.

While he was in New York, he was taken to watch a game of American football; one thing confused him. Asked afterwards how what he thought of it, he replied, *'Actually it is somewhat like rugby. But why do you have all these committee meetings?'*

At the end of his visit, in spite of his accident, he had very little to complain about. *'Toilet paper too thin, newspapers too fat,'* he told the Canadian press.

Back in Britain and now, in 1929, facing serious hardship, he knuckled down to his writing with even more vigour. About a year before, he had written to Baldwin that he'd had a *'delightful month'*, building a cottage and dictating a book – *'200 bricks & 2000 words per day'*: the cottage had been intended for the butler. Now the family moved into it, shutting up the house except for Churchill's study, which he continued to use.

With Ashley's help, and that of other assistants and secretaries, Churchill produced a phenomenal number of words published in books and articles, the latter, some 400 of them, printed in a number of different newspapers and journals. *'I write a book the way they built the Canadian Pacific Railway,'* he once said. *'First I lay the track from coast to coast, and then I put in all the stations.'* And, as he once said to Ashley, *'I aim to give the reader a good ride.'*

His readability ensured his popularity as an author – which in turn guaranteed that he would earn well by his writing. As he was by then receiving advances larger than those of many authors even today, he was able over time to recoup his losses. *'I kept my family by my pen,'* he declared; he also said that he lived *'from mouth to hand'*. During the ten years from 1929 his publications included the last volumes of *The World Crisis, My Early Life, India* (a collection of speeches on India), *Thoughts and Adventures* (a selection of essays), *Marlborough: His Life and Times* (four volumes), *Arms and the Covenant* (speeches) and *Step by Step 1936–1939*. By and large, his books were very well received, especially *My Early Life*, which brought him praise from his greatest political rivals: Austen Chamberlain rather tamely noted that 'Winston's *My Early Life* is very good reading'; Ramsay MacDonald, then Prime Minister, wrote to Churchill, 'You are an interesting cuss – I, a dull dog. May yours bring you both credit and cash.'

Ramsay MacDonald's praise for his book did nothing to soften Churchill's political insults. In January 1931, he attacked MacDonald's indecisiveness on trade union reform:

I remember, when I was a child, being taken to the celebrated Barnum's Circus, which contained an exhibition of freaks and monstrosities, but the exhibition on the programme which I most desired to see was one described as the 'Boneless Wonder'. My parents judged that spectacle would be too revolting and demoralizing for my young eyes, and I have waited fifty years to see the 'Boneless Wonder' on the Treasury Bench.

And, when the government had just been defeated by thirty votes, *'The greatest living master of falling without hurting himself'*, the Prime Minister, Ramsay MacDonald, rises *'utterly unabashed . . . and airily assures us that nothing has happened.'*

Not long after, Churchill resigned from the Conservative Business Committee (what would today be called the Shadow Cabinet) over the matter of independence for India.

One of Churchill's secretaries, Grace Hamblin, described how he would bring his visitors – and he had many, and of all kinds, from important political figures, to the literary and artistic, to friends of the family, young and old – to his office at Chartwell, where an assortment of people such as Maurice Ashley, various research assistants and his secretaries, would be working. Here, he would tell them, is *'my factory'*. Once, when there was only Grace Hamblin there, he announced to his guest, *'This is my factory . . . This is my secretary.'* After a pause he added dolefully, *'And to think I once commanded the fleet.'*

'Our rule in India is, as it were, a sheet of oil spread over and keeping free from storms a vast and profound ocean of humanity.' These words were Lord Randolph Churchill's, and his son felt the same way about the great sub-continent. In 1922, he had written to a friend, *'Our true duty in India lies to those 300 millions whose lives and means of existence would be squandered if entrusted to the chatterboxes who are supposed to speak for India today.'* Now the ruling Labour Party – with the support of Stanley Baldwin – was talking about giving India self-government.

At the time India was divided into 'British India', seventeen provinces under direct British administration, and over 500 other states ruled by Indian princes, except in the matter of interstate and international relations, which, among other things, were bound to support Britain in the event of a war. In the autumn of 1929, the Viceroy of India, Lord Irwin (to become Lord Halifax) had intimated that India would be granted Dominion status – that is, it would remain part of the British Empire, but would be self-governing. On 1 January 1930, India's nationalist party, the Indian National Congress declared that their goal was total independence. Churchill was appalled – how could India, so well looked after by the paternalistic British Empire, even consider self-rule, let alone complete independence, when there was so much potential for conflict between the many states without the discipline of British rule? India was not ready to rule herself. That a nation might prefer a rough ride at its own hands to a smooth ride under someone else's was incomprehensible to him. He also believed – and here he was not wrong – that much blood would be shed in the process. *'India is a geographical term. It is no more a united nation than the Equator,'* he once said.

Churchill launched himself into a campaign to persuade the largely pro-India Commons (many Conservatives supported the Labour and Liberal Members over giving India self-rule) to change their minds. Following a speech he made on 12 December 1930, Sir Francis Younghusband complained to *The Times*: 'Mr Churchill is never happy unless he is making a noise,' while Lord Irwin observed, 'What a monstrous speech Winston has just made.' A couple of days later Baldwin wrote to J. C. C. Davidson that 'Winston is very wild and has gone quite mad about India.' Even in an age when 'PC' meant police constable, and sensitivity to racial issues was slight, many were taken aback by Churchill's now famous reference to Mohandas Gandhi as *'a seditious Middle Temple lawyer, now posing as a fakir of a type well-known in the East, striding half-naked . . .'* In fact, the acrimony of the statement is more because Churchill knew that Gandhi had been accustomed, as a London-trained lawyer, to wearing smart Western-style clothing, and he felt that Gandhi's reversion to *'native costume'* was a pose and an act of betrayal towards the British who had nurtured him and trained him as a Middle Temple lawyer. Even so, it was uncalled for; he should have seen at the time that it was not a pose.

Although Victorian in his paternalism, he was not as racist as might appear – indeed when he was in South Africa, he tells us in *London to Ladysmith* (1900), he found himself arguing with a Boer who insisted that they, the Boers, knew 'how to treat Kaffirs . . . They were put here by the God Almighty to work for us. We'll stand no damned nonsense from them. We'll keep them in their proper places.' Churchill drew the conclusion that *'the true and original root of Dutch aversion to British rule . . . is the abiding fear and hatred of the movement that seeks to place the native on a level with the white man'.*

Later, indeed, although not happy about the newly granted Indian independence, Churchill did say to the Mahatma, *'I do not care whether you are more or less loyal to Great Britain . . . You need not expect anything but silence or help from us.'*

Over the years, Churchill continued to speak out against Indian independence, as well as other issues, including what he saw as the growing threat from Germany.

When the coalition National Government was formed in 1931, Ramsay MacDonald still Prime Minister, now with Baldwin as Deputy, Churchill was not offered a ministerial post. In 1933, he insisted that *'Further Indianization will ruin the great services without which India will fall back to the level of China'* (China was in a turmoil at the time, with some provinces under the control of the new national government, but most still ruled by warlords, while two groups of Communists were agitating for rebellion); Indian politicians were *'largely untried and provedly disloyal';* self-rule would, he said, *'darken the lives of the enormous mass of people'* in India. The Bill, he claimed, was *'a gigantic quilt of jumbled crochet work. There is no theme; there is no pattern; there is no agreement; there is no conviction; there is no simplicity; there is no courage.'*

On the other hand, Churchill did concede after the war that he had been wrong – in some respects. But he was right when he predicted that India's independence would result in the loss of many thousands of lives, as Hindu and Muslim and Sikh factions fought one another. Gandhi himself was deeply disappointed by the aftermath, saying to a journalist in 1947, 'Madam, you may write in your paper that India has never followed my way.' The following year he was assassinated by a fellow Hindu. Some of the bloodshed might well have been averted if Mountbatten had not hurried independence – and the partition of India, which he himself had recommended – through, before all boundary disputes had been settled, and evacuated British troops almost a year earlier than the target date. Churchill later told Mountbatten: *'What you did in India was like striking me across the face with your riding crop.'*

Mountbatten himself had a story to tell about Churchill and India, though not one involving his own actions. In 1942, in the middle of important discussions about the possibility of Allied landings in Europe, President Roosevelt had time to prepare a practical joke on Winston Churchill. He had found 'one of these American middle-aged crusading women', who was campaigning for the British to leave India and give her independence. A lunch at the White House had been arranged, with some eight or ten guests, one of them the crusading woman, who was seated next to Churchill, who was himself seated next to the President. While the other guests listened in gleeful anticipation, at the first possible opportunity the woman said: 'Mr Prime Minister, what do you intend to do about those wretched Indians?' Churchill, however, was unfazed. *'Madam,'* he responded, *'to which Indians do you refer? Do you by chance refer to the second greatest nation on earth, which under benign and beneficent British rule has multiplied and prospered exceedingly or do you mean those unfortunate Indians of the North American continent, which under your administration are practically extinct?'* Roosevelt and his co-conspirators had been hoist with their own petard – and by someone who believed himself to have *'Red Indian'* blood.

One advantage to being a backbench MP Churchill found was that he could criticize the government freely. As he was to say in 1947, *'When I am abroad, I always make it a rule never to criticize or attack the government of my own country. I make up for lost time when I get home.'* He attacked it on the matter of unemployment; on its financial policies; on socialism – *'Socialism is like a dream. Sooner or later you wake up to reality';* on what he saw as the demise of the Conservative party – 'Winston is in a state of violent defeatism,' Samuel Hoare told Lord Halifax, 'telling everyone that the Conservative party is destroyed for ever and that there is no hope of our getting back.'

There was also the matter of the Abdication Crisis in 1936, by which time Baldwin was Prime Minister again, where Churchill made, so to speak, a spectacle of himself in his efforts to stand up for Edward VIII, whom he felt was being forcibly hurried into abdication: 'He almost lost his head, and he certainly lost his command of the House. It was terribly dramatic,' wrote Harold Nicolson, MP.

> First we had Baldwin – slow and measured. Then Winston rose to ask a supplementary question. He failed to do it in the right form and was twice called to order by the Speaker. He hesitated and waved his spectacles vaguely in the air. 'Sit down,' they shouted. He waved his spectacles again and then collapsed.

Churchill had privately advised Edward VIII not to marry the American divorcee Mrs Simpson, and publicly he kept asking that the King be given more time. He also wrote to Baldwin, on 5 December, describing the great strain on the King and asking the Prime Minister to allow Edward more time to make a decision. The letter concludes, '*It would be a most cruel & wrong thing to extort a decision from him in his present state.*'

Two days later he demanded in the Commons for the third time that '*no irrevocable step be taken before the House had received a full statement*' from the King. The reaction was one of fury – 'one of the angriest manifestations I have ever heard directed against any man in the House of Commons,' according to Lord Winterton. And Churchill, for once unable to come up with a smart reply, burst out, '*You won't be satisfied until you've broken him, will you?*' and marched out of the House.

Robert Boothby, Churchill's friend and erstwhile Parliamentary Private Secretary, had his suspicions that Churchill was up to something, however, saying, according to Harold Nicolson's diary:

> I knew that Winston was going to do something dreadful. I had been staying the weekend with him. He was silent and restless and glancing into corners. Now when a dog does that, you know that he is about to be sick on the carpet. It is the same with Winston. He managed to hold it for three days, and then comes up to the House and is sick right across the floor . . .

He added: 'He has undone in five minutes the patient reconstruction work of two years.'

In the event, the King abdicated and married Mrs Simpson. The following year the Churchills attended the Coronation of King George VI. As Queen Elizabeth was being crowned, Churchill turned to Clementine and whispered, *'You were right. I see now that the "other one" wouldn't have done.'* Less than four years later, in 1941, he was having to concern himself with the former King – the Duke of Windsor – again, but things were very different now. The Duke had been in occupied France, and was now travelling in Spain and Portugal. His attitude to the Nazis was worrying – and they were showing too friendly an interest in him. To keep him well away from Britain and out of enemy hands he was appointed Governor of the Bahamas. Churchill advised him not to take *'a view of the war, or about the Germans, or about Hitlerism, which is different from that adopted by the British nation and Parliament'.*

Boothby's last comment about Churchill undoing patient reconstruction was a reference to Churchill's gradual return to acceptability in the eyes of his colleagues in the House of Commons and of the electorate in general, who, as time went by, had begun to feel that his warnings about Germany had a sound basis and that he might be a good person to have in government. Now he had apparently blown his credibility.

For years, as well as nagging the government about India and everything else he saw to criticize, Churchill had been especially vociferous in his warnings about Germany and condemnation of the British government's unreadiness for war. In 1924, in an article for *Nash's Pall Mall*, 'Shall We All Commit Suicide?', he had written: *'The story of the human race is War. Except for brief and precarious interludes, there has never been peace in the world; and before history began, murderous strife was universal and unending.'* Ten years later he was telling the nation much the same thing in a BBC broadcast – that war was universal and had been going on since well before weapons were invented. True as those words were, nobody wanted to be told. They'd had the Great War – that was enough to end all wars, look at how so many had been killed, so many had suffered; then look at the negotiations that had culminated in the Treaty of Versailles, which had effectively emasculated Germany, the nation that was to blame for the Great War. Europe was at peace as a result. When the Admiralty mentioned the territorial and economic ambitions of Japan, the suggestion was pooh-poohed even by Churchill.

But he was made nervous by all the talk of disarmament. In 1928, he diverted his constituents with his simplistic 'Disarmament Fable', which depicted the problems that can arise when the decision is made to ban certain weapons but allow others without somehow providing for general security; the animals in the fable have this vital general security in the shape of the zoo keepers. In the real, human world, zoo keepers would not be acceptable.

> *Once upon a time all the animals in the Zoo decided that they would disarm, and they arranged to have a conference to settle the matter. So the Rhinoceros said when he opened the proceedings that the use of teeth was barbarous and horrible and ought to be strictly prohibited by general consent. Horns, which were mainly defensive weapons, would, of course, have to be allowed. The Buffalo, the Stag, the Porcupine, and even*

the little Hedgehog all said they would vote with the Rhino, but the Lion and the Tiger took a different view. They defended teeth and even claws, which they described as honourable weapons of immemorial antiquity. The Panther, the Leopard, the Puma, and the whole tribe of small cats all supported the Lion and the Tiger.

Then the Bear spoke. He proposed that both teeth and horns should be banned and never used again for fighting by any animal. It would be quite enough if animals were allowed to give each other a good hug when they quarrelled. No one could object to that. It was so fraternal, and that would be a great step towards peace. However, all the other animals were very offended with the Bear, and the Turkey fell into a perfect panic.

The discussion got so hot and angry, and all those animals began thinking so much about horns and teeth and hugging when they argued about the peaceful intentions that had brought them together that they began to look at one another in a very nasty way. Luckily the keepers were able to calm them down and persuade them to go back quietly to their cages, and they began to feel quite friendly with one another again.

Europe had no keepers – the League of Nations lacked the capability to enforce its own recommendations to be zoo keepers. Churchill would probably have liked to see himself as one – a paternal authoritarian figure dispensing reason and justice. It would have fitted in with his romanticized images – the little boy dancing round the classroom declaiming, the dashing young officer galloping through a rain of bullets, the cloaked figure leaping up to direct traffic, the other cloaked figure calmly smoking his cigar in the midst of flying shrapnel. A benign dictator. As he remarked in 1926: *'I am not invested with dictatorial powers. If I were, I should be quite ready to dictate.'*

Chapter 7

Churchill's Feeling for War

I N 1929, referring specifically to the situation in China where Chinese warlords were threatening British interests, but surely with dark stirrings in Europe in mind too, Churchill wrote to Baldwin:

> . . . there is no evil worse than submitting to wrong and violence for fear of war. Once you take the position of not being able in any circumstance to defend your rights against the aggression of some particular set of people, there is no end to the demands that will be made upon you or to the humiliations that must be accepted.

But China was far away, and the Versailles Treaty, signed ten years before, had ensured peace for Europe, hadn't it? Not all thought so: France's Marshal Ferdinand Foch with uncannily precise prediction remarked 'this is not a peace treaty, it is an armistice for twenty years' (he did not live to see the truth of his words), and neither had Churchill been in favour of the treaty. His friend Victor Cazalet noted in 1922: 'Apropos of the Versailles Treaty, Winston told me he said at the time to LG that he would not put his name to it for

1,000 pounds.' This seems a bit early for it to have been hindsight on Churchill's part, unless he had in mind the recently formed National Socialist German Workers' Party (NSDAP – to become the Nazi Party) that in early 1920 had published its first programme with its '25 Points', which rejected outright the terms of the Treaty of Versailles.

The swingeing penalties that were imposed on Germany by the Treaty were, quite simply, too much for that nation to put up with – she was stripped of her colonies abroad; some territories (including those with a substantial proportion of her mineral resources and industries, along with their population) were taken from her, importation, exportation and nearly all production of military weapons was prohibited; strict limitations were imposed upon her armed forces, and she was expected to pay war reparations as well; the humiliation alone was bad enough. At the time of the signing of the treaty, Germany saw the terms as unacceptable, and as France's revenge, but initially there were no thoughts of aggression and rearming. The Centre Party newspaper, *Germania*, wrote:

> From now onwards not a day must pass in which it is not repeated in the German Press, including even the smallest of the provincial papers: 'The Peace Treaty must be revised! The protest against it must be made permanently. Our hatred must be fraternity. Our revenge must be love which will destroy hatred! Our hope must be faith in ourselves and our children!' . . . We reject all bloodthirsty screaming for revenge. The German people must again come to its senses and manifest its solidarity, and first and foremost by the care and practice of real culture.

Even before the Treaty was signed (June 1919), France was not happy. She wanted the area west of the Rhine that had once belonged to her – rather than a demilitarized German Rhineland, even if it was occupied by the Allies. The French President Raymond Poincaré wrote in his diary in March 1919:

Today Clemenceau [the Prime Minister] is angry with the English, and especially with Lloyd George. 'I won't budge,' he said. I will act like a hedgehog and wait until they come to talk to me. I will yield nothing. We will see if they can manage without me. Lloyd George is a trickster . . . Lloyd George said to me, 'Well, now that we are going to disarm Germany, you no longer need the Rhine.' I said to Clemenceau: 'Does disarmament then seem to him to give the same guarantees? Does he think that, in the future, we can be sure of preventing Germany from rebuilding her army?'

It was not long before trouble did arise between France and Germany, in the form of border disputes, France being determined that every term of the Treaty should be strictly adhered to. When France requested Britain's help, Churchill, then Chancellor of the Exchequer, unwilling to support all the terms of the Treaty, suggested that France should *'stew in her own juice'*, at least until some agreement was arrived at, and *'rectification'* of Germany's borders was implemented. *'This war,'* he said in 1925, *'which has occurred between France and Germany several times, has broken up the world. What guarantee have we got while things are going as they are that we shall not have another war? In fact, it seems as if we were moving towards it, although it may not be for twenty years, certainly not until Germany acquire some methods of waging war, chemically or otherwise.'* Mr Churchill had a feeling for war.

Clearly, the Versailles Treaty had a lot to answer for. *'In those days,'* Churchill said to the House in 1938, *'I ventured repeatedly to submit to the House the maxim that the grievances of the vanquished should be redressed before the disarmament of the victors was begun. But the reverse was done.'* A 1925 article in *The Times* commented on how, in the Treaty, 'In every chapter, almost every clause, we have the clear distinction between the victors and the vanquished – the Allied and Associated Powers still acting as an organized body, imposing their will relentlessly upon Germany and the other defeated countries. This is no peace; it is merely the perpetuation of war!'

In 1949, Churchill was to say, *'The idea that the vanquished could pay the expenses of the victors was a destructive and crazy delusion.'* And he reiterated, in *The Second World War: The Gathering Storm*, *'The redress of the grievances of the vanquished should precede the disarmament of the victors.'*

In the event, the Treaties of Locarno – seven agreements, the first signed in October 1925, intended to uphold the security of western Europe, mostly by guaranteeing the common boundaries in continental Europe and providing for the arbitration of disputes between neighbouring countries – helped to calm the situation temporarily, and plans for disarmament went on. Yet, in 1930 – before Hitler was in power – Churchill, after a meeting with a German diplomat, reported to the Foreign Office that *'Hitler has declared he has no intention of waging a war of aggression. I, however, am convinced that Hitler, or his followers, will seize the first available opportunity to resort to armed force.'* And, a year later, he wrote in an article, *'Surely, the mastery of Hitlerism by the constitutional forces in Germany will be a real factor in the peace of Europe.'*

In 1932 Churchill went to Germany, where he didn't meet Hitler, despite the strenuous efforts of the Nazi Party's Foreign Press Chief, Ernst Hanfstängl, a half-American, half-German Harvard graduate, who had fallen under Hitler's spell when he had heard him speak at a Munich beer hall in 1921, and had become an ardent supporter. His job now was to improve Hitler's image overseas and, no doubt aware of Churchill's estimation of his boss, he was anxious that they should meet and Churchill revise his opinion. What followed had a distinct element of farce about it.

Churchill was staying at an hotel in Munich, with his son Randolph, daughter Sarah, and Professor Lindemann; Hitler used to stay at the same hotel, and there the Churchill party became friendly with 'Putzi' Hanfstängl, who entertained them by playing the piano and singing English songs. *'He said I ought to meet* [Hitler], *and that nothing would be easier to arrange. Herr Hitler . . . would be very glad indeed to see me,'* Churchill wrote in *The Second World War: The Gathering Storm. 'I had no national prejudices against Hitler at this time. I knew little of his doctrine and nothing of his character. I admire men who stand up for their own country in defeat, even though I was on the other side.'* (He in fact knew enough about Hitler by 1930 to issue the warning to the Foreign Office quoted above.)

The meeting was not at all easy to arrange. Hanfstängl went off to invite Hitler to join the Churchill party at dinner. 'Don't they realize how busy I am? What on earth would I talk to [Churchill] about?' Hitler snapped at him. Hanfstängl returned to Churchill and his companions, telling them that Hitler might join them for coffee; he perhaps relayed the second half of Hitler's reply, because Churchill said to him, *'There are a few questions you might like to put to him, which can be the basis of our discussion when we meet.'* One of these was, *'What is the sense of being against a man simply because of his birth? How can any man help how he is born?'* He added, *'Tell your boss from me that anti-Semitism may be a good starter, but it is a bad sticker.'*

He also asked, *'How does your chief feel about an alliance between your country, France and England?'* A coalition of this sort would have been welcomed by the British government as a way of preventing war and redressing some of Germany's grievances – but Churchill must have known that, apart from the fact that Hitler was not yet in the position to do so, the likelihood of him agreeing to such a pact was slim indeed.

Hanfstängl set off back to Hitler. He found his boss, he wrote in his memoirs, 'in a dirty white overcoat, just saying good-bye to a Dutchman . . . "Herr Hitler . . . don't you realize the Churchills are sitting in the restaurant? . . . They are expecting you for coffee and will think this a deliberate insult."' Hitler said he was unshaven and had too much to do. Hanfstängl suggested he shave and come anyway, and returned to the Churchill party, where he stayed on, playing the piano for them, in the hope that Hitler would eventually turn up. He didn't.

Hanfstängl later concluded that Hitler did 'not have the social guts' to meet Churchill.

By the following year, Hanfstängl had become

disillusioned with Hitler and the Nazi Party, and following a number of disagreements was pushed to the outer fringes of the party. By 1937, Hitler suspected enough disloyalty in him to get rid of him by dropping him from a plane into hostile territory. The pilot, who knew of the plot, told Hanfstängl, and then, claiming engine trouble, made an emergency landing, allowing his passenger to escape. After further adventures Hanfstängl eventually spent the war in Washington, DC, on the other side, as a political and psychological warfare adviser to the United States.

An interesting addendum to this is another story about Hanfstängl and Hitler . . . In November 1923, Hitler took 600 armed storm troopers and marched on a beer hall in Munich where a right-wing political meeting was taking place. His plan, in brief, was to seize power and establish a new regime over Germany, with the popular First World War veteran General Ludendorff as dictator. The plan failed and the Nazi supporters took flight. Hanfstängl fled to Austria, but – so the story goes – curiously enough, Hitler took refuge in Hanfstängl's home, where Hanfstängl's beautiful wife hid him. When the police arrived to search the house, Hitler, it seems, put a loaded revolver to his head, and it was only thanks to Frau Hanfstängl's persuasive powers that he did not kill himself there and then. Instead, he was arrested, and spent nine months in prison, during which time support for him grew, and he dictated *Mein Kampf* to Rudolf Hess. It would be interesting, if futile, to speculate what might have happened if she had let him kill himself, assuming the story to be true.

*

In the meantime, Churchill continued to sound off against Hitler and the British failure to rearm. The efforts of the League of Nations and negotiations for peace in Europe without rearming, he felt, were pointless. In 1933, he gave a speech to the Royal Society of St George (on 24 April, as St George's Day, the 23rd, fell on a Sunday), regaling his audience with one of his little stories.

> *I have to speak to you about St George and the Dragon. I have been wondering what would happen if that legend were repeated under modern conditions.*
>
> *St George would arrive in Cappadocia, accompanied not by a horse, but by a secretariat. He would be armed not with a lance, but with several flexible formulas. He would, of course, be welcomed by the local branch of the League of Nations Union. He would propose a conference with the Dragon – a Round Table Conference, no doubt – that would be more convenient for the Dragon's tail. He would make a trade agreement with the Dragon. He would lend the Dragon a lot of money for the Cappadocian taxpayers. The maiden's release would be referred to Geneva, the Dragon reserving all his rights meanwhile. Finally St George would be photographed with the Dragon (inset – the maiden).*

He made sure, too, that he knew what was going on. Desmond Morton, Director of the Industrial Intelligence Centre, who lived in Edenbridge, a few miles from Chartwell, was a useful neighbour, his job being to find out what Germany was up to in the way of rearmament; further information, this time about Britain's air defences, came from Squadron Leader Torr Anderson, while Ralph Wigram, an official at the

Foreign Office, also helped keep Churchill informed. The danger of a German airborne attack was an overriding concern, indeed Churchill was accused of having a bee in his bonnet about it, but in November 1934 he did at least persuade Baldwin to see to it that the government would ensure that the strength of the Royal Air Force would not fall below that of the Luftwaffe, the German airforce that had been secretly built up. In 1935 he was appointed to a secret committee on air defence research, and involved himself in the build-up of the RAF. As he once said, *'We have never been likely to get into trouble by having an extra thousand or two of up-to-date aeroplanes at our disposal.'*

In January 1933, Hitler became Chancellor; in April, Churchill was warning, *'The rise of Germany . . . to anything like military equality with France, Poland or the small states, means a renewal of a general European war.'* Later that year, Ramsay MacDonald announced the government's disarmament plans to the House. In 1934, Churchill warned of a nation where *'the philosophy of blood lust is being inculcated into their youth in a manner unparalleled since the days of barbarism'*; in a BBC broadcast he spoke of a nation, *'which with all its strength and virtue is in the grip of a group of ruthless men preaching a gospel of intolerance and racial pride unrestrained by law by Parliament or by public opinion'.*

In the summer of 1934, the corrupt and dictatorial Governor of Louisiana, the 'Kingfish' Huey Long was assassinated. Churchill greeted this with satisfaction and a glance in Hitler's direction (and Mussolini's): *'The Louisiana Dictator has met his fate. Sic semper tyrannis, which means "so perish all who do the like again". This*

*was the most clownish of the Dictator tribe. Let us hope
that more serious tyrants will also lose their sway.'*

Not long after, a Labour motion of censure against the
government's increasing Britain's air power was defeated
decisively. *'The Socialists wish us to remain disarmed,
but exceedingly abusive about Germany,'* scoffed
Churchill.

Gradually people were beginning to listen to
Churchill, as events in Germany began to suggest that he
might have a sound basis for his warnings. His hopes
were raised when the general election in November led
to the Lord President, Stanley Baldwin, MacDonald's
deputy, being granted the premiership – but: 'Don't put
Winston in the Government,' Nancy Astor said to
Baldwin. 'It will mean war at home *and* abroad.'
Baldwin, however, said to colleagues, 'If there is going to
be war . . . we must keep him fresh to be our war Prime
Minister.'

Stanley Baldwin became Prime Minister in June
1935, and Churchill did not forgive his old friend for not
offering him a Cabinet post; he had hoped to be, once
again, First Lord. He continued to inveigh against the
granting of independence to India and against the
British government's lack of preparedness for war. *'In
those days,'* he declared, harking back to his time as
Chancellor, Baldwin *'was wiser than he is now; he used
frequently to take my advice.'* For his part, Baldwin said,
'When Winston was born lots of fairies swooped down
on his cradle with gifts – imagination, eloquence, industry, ability; and then came a fairy who said, "No one
person has the right to so many gifts", picked him up and
gave him such a shake and twist that with all the gifts he
was denied judgement and wisdom.'

In the summer of 1936, Churchill, Austen Chamberlain and Lord Salisbury led a parliamentary deputation to Baldwin on the need for rearmament. Baldwin's answer was that there was a strong pacifist feeling in the country. 'People will only learn, unfortunately, in a democracy, by butting their heads against a brick wall,' he pronounced, pointing out the difficulty in 'scaring the people without scaring them into fits'.

Baldwin's view was that Germany would strike east not west – and to him a confrontation between Nazis and Bolsheviks was not a cause for concern – and he believed that rearmament would only frighten the peace-loving British electorate into believing that the government was spoiling for war. So, refusing to recognize how important it was that Britain should show herself to be fully ready to fight if the need to defend herself arose, he did nothing. Churchill's reaction, unleashed during a Commons debate on 12 November, was one of unbridled scorn: *'The Government cannot make up their minds, or they cannot get the Prime Minister to make up his mind. So they go on, in strange paradox, decided only to be undecided, resolved to be irresolute, adamant for drift, solid for fluidity, all-powerful to be impotent.'* His fury was aimed at Baldwin in particular, who Churchill was sure knew but would not acknowledge the danger from Germany: *'Occasionally he stumbled over the truth, but hastily picked himself up and hurried on as if nothing had happened'* and – descending to crude personal insult: *'He is no better than an epileptic corpse.'*

Baldwin's inclination was to concentrate on what was going on in Britain (according to Lord Halifax, at the time of the Abdication crisis the Prime Minister said, 'I foresee that I shall have a lot of trouble over this. I hope that you will not bother me with foreign affairs during the next three months') and avoid involvement in foreign affairs through a policy of non-intervention (as in the case of the Spanish Civil War) and of appeasement. Thus in 1935 when Italy invaded Abyssinia (Ethiopia), he sent Sir Samuel Hoare, now Secretary of State for Foreign Affairs, to draw up, with the French Premier and Minister for Foreign Affairs, Pierre Laval (who was later to head the collaborationist wartime Vichy government and ultimately be executed for treason), an agreement which granted to Italy some two-thirds of Abyssinia, the idea being to maintain a front against Germany through an alliance with Italy. When Baldwin was asked in Cabinet whether there should not be some discussion before irrevocable decisions were made, he said, 'I think we all have confidence in Sam; we can safely leave it in his hands.' Details of the Hoare-Laval Pact were leaked to the press, which led to an outburst of public indignation, in both France and Britain, and it was rejected by both countries. The Laval government fell; Hoare was forced to resign.

Churchill, it is said, was asked by someone, referring to the 'Abyssinia Crisis': 'Don't you think it is high time that the British Lion showed its teeth?' Disconsolately viewing the state of Britain's defences, he replied, '*It must go to the dentist first.*' He was away at the time and was advised by friends to stay away 'because you will be in a unique position of strength since you will neither have supported the Government, compromised yourself by hostility, nor taken the negative though semi-hostile line of abstention'. Churchill was known not to be a fan of Samuel Hoare.

He was by now no longer a fan of Mussolini, either, whose '*Roman genius*' he had praised in 1933. In 1937, he commented, '*The danger from which we suffer is that Mussolini thinks all can be carried off by bluff and bullying, and that in the end we shall only blether and withdraw.*' And in 1938, in an article entitled 'Dictators on Dynamite', he compared the two dictators:

> *Hitler is an instrument of destiny. He embodies the revolt of Germany against the hard fortune of war, the soul-compelling surge of a warrior nation against defeat, its passion for rehabilitation and revenge. He exemplifies and enshrines the will of Germany . . . Signor Mussolini is not the prisoner nor the instrument of forces outside himself. He follows no path but his own. He uses the events and circumstances of post-war Italy as he would have used those of any other clime and century.*

When, in the summer of 1936, the fighting between the democratically elected moderate socialist government of Spain, the Republican, supported by far-left and communist groups, and the growing Fascist party (with the backing of a group of military leaders) erupted into civil war, both factions looked to the rest of Europe for support. The French Premier Léon Blum was on the point of sending aid to the Republicans, but was quickly discouraged on the grounds that intervention might spark off an international war, given the rising tensions in Europe. Even Churchill urged strict neutrality – though privately he said to Clementine, '*I am thankful the Spanish Nationalists are making progress . . . better for the safety of all if the Communists are crushed.*' But he recognized the danger presented by Franco as well, seeing that victory for either Nationalists or Communists could only lead to '*a prolonged period of iron rule*'.

Mussolini and Hitler, however, had no qualms about sending aid to the Nationalist – or Fascist – Party, and even after twenty-seven countries, including Italy and Germany, had signed a non-intervention pact, they continued to send military equipment to Franco. Like Churchill, Hitler admired Mussolini's achievement in restoring order and economic stability to a country that had been crippled by a general strike. But while Churchill soon stopped admiring Mussolini, Hitler sought a closer relationship with him, and in October 1936 they signed a non-military alliance. Three years later, soon after Italy had occupied Albania in April 1939, they signed a full defensive alliance (the Pact of Steel) – in spite of which Mussolini did not come into the war against the Allies until June 1940, when he believed that Nazi Germany was winning the war and thought it expedient to join in and share in the glory and profits. Italy was ill-equipped, and when they tried to invade Greece through Albania, German troops had to come to their aid. This led to Italy becoming subordinate to Nazi Germany, while Greece and Crete fell to the Nazis. Churchill was scathing in a 1941 speech:

> *Here surely is the world's record in the domain of the ridiculous and contemptible. This whipped jackal, Mussolini, who to save his own skin has made all Italy a vassal state of Hitler's Empire, comes frisking up at the side of the German tiger with yelpings not only of appetite – that can be understood – but even of triumph.*

In 1945 Churchill was to call the Second World War an *'unnecessary war'*, and one that could have easily been prevented. In 1938, he pointed out in a broadcast to the States, published in *The Times* for home consumption, that had Hitler been faced by *'a formidable array of peace-defending powers . . . this would have been an opportunity for all peace-loving and moderate forces in Germany, together with the German army, to make a great effort to re-establish something like sane and civilized conditions in their country.'* Whether generating and organizing a formidable array of peace-defending powers would have been feasible is not certain – especially given the rise of Mussolini – and to rely on the 'peace-loving and moderate forces' within an enemy country might seem a trifle risky, but as it was, Britain was vulnerable enough for Hitler to recognize the fact and use it to encourage his military forces.

In 1937 Churchill published *Great Contemporaries*, a collection of essays on important figures of his day. They were not necessarily people he entirely admired, but he believed them to be great because, as he said, *'The characteristic of a great man is his power to leave a lasting impression on people he meets.'* It included an article on Hitler that he had published in the *Strand* magazine in 1935, which is particularly interesting as he was careful to give Hitler credit where he felt that credit was due. He expressed admiration for Hitler's achievements: *'One may dislike Hitler's system and yet admire his patriotic achievement. If our country were defeated, I hope we should find a champion as admirable to restore our courage and lead us back to our place among the nations.'* The story of Hitler's *'struggle cannot be read without admiration for the courage, the perseverance, and the vital force which enabled him to challenge, defy, conciliate, or overcome, all the authorities or resistances which barred his path . . . Thus the world lives on hopes that the worst is over, and that we may yet live to see Hitler a gentler figure in a happier age.'*

Churchill's earlier words about Hitler, and his dire warnings, suggest that he did not believe the last sentence, but perhaps that he would have liked to. Most people in Europe would have been content with a 'gentle' Hitler and a happy age, and hoped that this would come about once the German Chancellor had managed to restore his country to prosperity, without recourse to war. *'Because the story is unfinished we must never forget nor cease to hope for the bright alternative.'* It sounds too much like wishful thinking. By 1935 Churchill was well aware that Hitler represented a grave danger to Europe, but by presenting a balanced view he was perhaps hoping to reach the general peace-loving public and to show that peace was what he too sought – and that he believed peace was only achievable by building up enough defences to deter Germany from any further acts of aggression. For, the article continues:

Recently he has offered many words of reassurance, eagerly lapped up by those who have been so tragically wrong about Germany in the past. Only time can show, but, meanwhile, the great wheels revolve; the rifles, the cannon, the tanks, the shot and shell, the air-bombs, the poison gas cylinders, the aeroplanes, the submarines, and now the beginnings of a fleet flow in ever-broadening streams from the already largely war-mobilized arsenals and factories of Germany.

Even this passage – with its list of all that Germany had been manufacturing in direct contravention of the Versailles Treaty – is relatively moderate, its factual tone more convincing to those who resisted Churchill's rantings. But he was also strongly condemnatory of Hitler's treatment of Jews – indeed, even earlier, in April 1933, he warned, *'There is a danger of the odious conditions now ruling in Germany, being extended by conquest to Poland and another persecution and pogrom of Jews being begun in this new area.'* In the essay on Franklin D. Roosevelt in *Great Contemporaries*, he referred to the *'petty persecutions and old-world assertions of brutality in which the German idol* [Hitler] *has indulged'*.

By 1936 Churchill was receiving closer attention at home and abroad, but the majority of those in power still did not take his warnings seriously. His outburst in the Commons in December, over the King's abdication, did not help his case. His daughter, Lady Soames, later wrote 'now discredit was cast on him by the feeling that his support of the King sprang from ulterior motives, and was largely prompted by antipathy to Baldwin'.

Shortly before, Baldwin had said:

> Supposing I had . . . said that Germany was rearming and that we must rearm, does anybody think that this pacific democracy would have rallied to that cry at that moment? I cannot think of anything that would have made the loss of the election from my point of view more certain.

That Baldwin should by his own admission have refused to rearm for fear of losing the election cost him the support of many, and Churchill was beginning to be seen as a possible replacement for him. However, Churchill's outburst in the King's defence was seen as an attempt to shake the already fragile structure of Baldwin's premiership and bring him down – and this lost *him* some support . . . while Baldwin's acknowledgement that he had been wrong about not rearming was seen as commendable honesty. In the event, Baldwin handled the Abdication crisis with wisdom and dignity; he retired in May 1937, was created the 1st Earl Baldwin of Bewdley, and almost immediately vanished from public life. Churchill welcomed with gloom the appointment of Neville Chamberlain as Prime Minister, announcing to Clementine that he was going to retire from politics.

He did not retire from politics, but as the storm clouds gathered he continued his gadfly behaviour with increased vigour. He and Chamberlain agreed over one thing: that Britain was militarily weaker than Germany. Chamberlain, however, believed that war could be avoided through appeasement – *'He has a lust for peace,'* Churchill complained. He was later to write, in the first volume of *The Second World War*:

> [Chamberlain's] *all-pervading hope was to go down in history as the Great Peacemaker; and for this he was prepared to strive continually in the teeth of facts . . . In those closing years before the war, I should have found it easier to work with Baldwin, as I knew him, than with Chamberlain; but neither of them had any wish to work with me except in the last resort.*

But, as Churchill remarked after Baldwin had left office (invoking an image of a Halloween pumpkin, its light extinguished), *'The candle in that great turnip has gone out.'* The opportunity to work with him again was not to arise. The turnip did, however, reiterate in a letter to a friend in 1938, 'W is a very forceful character and if war should come, the country will want him to lead them.'

Some years later, during the Blitz, a German bomb fell on Baldwin's house, which on hearing about the incident Churchill joked, *'What base ingratitude.'* The following year, however, by which time the public had well and truly condemned Baldwin as one of the 'Guilty Men' responsible for the war, and deliberately made a beeline for the ornate iron gates of Baldwin's country house (iron being collected for use in armaments factories), Churchill recognized that they were acting out of ill will in the guise of collecting for the war effort and told them to lay off – unfortunately for Baldwin without success.

Churchill's relationship with Baldwin remained ambivalent. When asked in 1947 if he was sending eightieth-birthday greetings to Baldwin, he famously responded: *'I wish Stanley Baldwin no ill, but it would have been much better if he had never lived.'* It would have sufficed to say that he wished Baldwin had never entered politics, surely? He cannot have forgotten that Baldwin gave him the much-coveted office of Chancellor of the Exchequer (in the days when Baldwin *'was wiser than he is now'*, when he used to take Churchill's advice). He did not wish Baldwin dead, though; Baldwin died a few months later.

Asked in 1938 how prepared Britain should be for war, Churchill answered with a story of a man who received a telegram from Brazil telling him his mother-in-law was dead and asking for instructions. He replied: *'Embalm, cremate, bury at sea. Take no chances.'* It would seem that Chamberlain in his quest for peace was also trying to take no chances.

In February 1938 the Foreign Secretary, Anthony Eden, who opposed Chamberlain's policy of appeasement, resigned in protest, and was replaced by Lord Halifax (the former Viceroy of India), who fully supported appeasement.

A month later Hitler annexed Austria and laid claim to the Sudetenland, a region of Czechoslovakia with a large ethnic German population. That same month, the French Prime Minister, Léon Blum, newly returned to office, called for an end to non-intervention (France was bound by treaty to aid Czechoslovakia should she be attacked) and Chamberlain supported France's right wing in ousting him from office. In April Chamberlain signed an agreement with Italy recognizing Italian rule in Abyssinia.

In the meantime Hitler continued to press for the Sudetenland, claiming that the Sudeten Germans were being discriminated against by the Czech government – *'the most pampered minority in Europe,'* Churchill called them. (No mention was made by the Nazis of the Sudetenland's vast economic resources.) A series of negotiations began on the ceding of the Sudetenland to Germany – but in early August, the Foreign Office received intelligence from the British Military Attaché in Berlin that Hitler had decided to attack Czechoslovakia whatever concessions were made to the Sudeten Germans. It was nevertheless decided that the way to avoid war would be to persuade Czechoslovakia to make enough concessions to ensure that Hitler would have no excuse to attack.

On 15 September Chamberlain flew to Berchtesgaden, Hitler's private retreat in Bavaria, to talk with the German Chancellor. That same day, Churchill told the *Daily Telegraph* that '*From the moment that German troops attempt to cross the Czechoslovakian frontier, the whole scene will be transformed and a roar of fury will arise from the free peoples of the world, which will proclaim nothing less than a crusade against the aggressor.*' Churchill flew to Paris on 20 September with his friend, the bilingual General Spears (originally 'Spiers'), to talk (unofficially) to the two most strongly anti-Nazi members of the French Cabinet, and on his return the next day announced to the press that a surrender to the Nazi threat of force would bring, not peace or safety, but ever-increasing weakness and danger.

Chamberlain, back in Britain, had in the meantime been visited by the French Premier, Édouard Daladier and his Foreign Minister, Georges Bonnet, after which he went back to Germany on the 22nd, returned two days later, less than happy with Hitler, but on the 28th was happy to hurry back to Munich for a four-power conference.

On 29 September the Munich Agreement, securing the Sudetenland for Germany, was signed by Britain, France, Germany and Italy. Chamberlain arrived back in Britain triumphantly waving his 'peace with honour' bit of paper. '*An old town clerk looking at European affairs through the wrong end of a municipal drainpipe,*' growled Churchill (referring to Chamberlain's earlier days – in municipal government as Lord Mayor of Birmingham).

'Peace in our time,' Chamberlain declared. 'I have always been of the opinion that if we could get a peaceful solution to the Czechoslovak question it would open the way generally to appeasement in Europe,' he announced joyously. '. . . We regard the agreement signed last night . . . as symbolic of the desire of our two peoples never to go to war with one another again.' All parties involved had been polite and complimentary towards each other (it is interesting to speculate what it might have been like had Churchill been there), and, commented *The Times*, 'In general, the Agreement is regarded here as a triumph of common sense and good will.'

Churchill did not share the Prime Minister's euphoria, and attacked him bitterly in Parliament: *'You were given the choice between war and dishonour. You chose dishonour and you will have war.'* He knew that Hitler would not be satisfied with just the Sudetenland. *'We have sustained a defeat without a war,'* he said, *'. . . do not suppose that this is the end. This is only the beginning of the reckoning. This is only the first sip, the first foretaste of a bitter cup . . .'*

A couple of months later, during a debate on Palestine, Malcolm MacDonald, Secretary of State for the Colonies, had reached the end of a difficult speech and was discoursing lyrically about the land itself: 'Bethlehem, where the Prince of Peace was born . . .'

Churchill's voice broke in: *'Bethlehem? I thought Neville was born in Birmingham.'*

Chapter 8

Winston Is Back

I N THE FIRST WORLD WAR a pilot in the Royal
Flying Corps won the Military Cross. His name was
Malcolm Christie and, clear as his loyalty to Britain was,
he, most usefully, had been educated in Germany. He
served as an air attaché in Berlin, and in 1930 started a
business career there. He had connections with British
Intelligence and, on a freelance basis, spied on
Germany, using as a base a house he owned on the
German–Dutch border. He knew Göring, and was a
close friend of Göring's deputy in the Reich Air
Ministry, Field Marshal Erhard Milch; he also associated with anti-Nazi German politicians, from whom he
gleaned much useful information, some (if not all) of
which made its way to Churchill's ears.

In 1936 Christie was passing on to the British
government detailed information concerning aircraft
production in Germany and the long-term plans for the
Luftwaffe. He also warned that there were plans to
invade the Rhineland, and, following a talk with Göring
in early February 1937, he urgently reported that
Germany's intention was to take control of Austria and
Czechoslovakia.

Christie's reports were widely circulated in Whitehall but do not seem to have been acted upon in any decisive manner. Churchill's warning speeches and articles, however, reflected many of Christie's warnings. And while no one could ever have accused Churchill of not being sure of himself, perhaps his certainty about what Germany was going to do was fuelled by Christie's reports – along with the intelligence he was receiving from Desmond Morton and others. Clearly, he granted the reports greater credence than did the more cautious government, which preferred no doubt not to look too hard for anything that might upset their plans for peace.

In March 1938 Christie told the British government that if Britain joined forces with Czechoslovakia against Germany, Hitler could be ousted – but, he warned that they would have to act quickly. The 'crucial question is "How soon will the next step against Czechoslovakia be tried?" . . . The probability is that the delay will not exceed two or three months at most, unless France and England provide the deterrent, for which cooler heads in Germany are praying.'

But Chamberlain would not accept this information and signed the Munich Agreement in September. Less than a year later, in August 1939, he was to receive another warning from Christie – that Hitler was planning an attack against Poland, imminently. Once again Neville Chamberlain did not act on the information.

In the meantime, following the Munich Agreement, Churchill had simply to continue to speak out against Chamberlain's policies, to continue being accused of warmongering. His anti-Nazi diatribes did not escape

Hitler who, in a speech in Munich on 8 November 1938 remarked, 'Mr Churchill may have an electorate of 15,000 or 20,000. I have one of 40 million. Once and for all we request to be spared being spanked like a pupil by a governess.'

The Nazi leader, of course, continued to help himself – as Churchill said, the *'totalitarian tigers'* had insatiable appetites, and the more they had, the more they wanted. (*'The German dictator, instead of snatching the victuals from the table, has been content to have them served to him course by course,'* Churchill said on 5 October.)

In March 1939 Hitler cocked a snook at the Munich Agreement and occupied the rest of Czechoslovakia – easily done as the Munich Pact had lost for Czechoslovakia two borders, and with them its most important fortifications and natural defences. Churchill, who was at the time working on his massive *History of the English-Speaking Peoples*, was heard to remark to a guest at dinner, *'It's hard to take one's attention off the events of today and concentrate on the reign of James II, but I am going to do it.'* No doubt he did, too – his secretaries and assistants have testified to his orderly methods of working, and remarked on how he was able to concentrate fully on the job in hand until it was time to switch over to something else, often completely different, upon which he would then concentrate as fully.

Poor Chamberlain at last had to recognize that Hitler could not be trusted – he had, he complained, been wretchedly betrayed. *'The high belief in the perfection of man,'* commented Churchill, *'is appropriate in a man of the cloth, but not in a prime minister.'*

Before Chamberlain was due to address her local Conservative Association, the Duchess of Buccleuch, asked Churchill where he thought she should have the podium set up. *'It doesn't matter where you put it,'* he replied with sardonic gloom, *'as long as he has the sun in his eyes and the wind in his teeth.'*

He now warned, *'It seems to me that Hitler will not stop short of the Black Sea unless arrested by the threat of a general war, or actual hostilities.'* The most that Britain did at this stage, however, was to guarantee to Poland that Britain would come to her aid should Germany threaten Polish independence.

Churchill was now urging Britain to make an alliance with the USSR, much as he distrusted the Bolsheviks, recognizing that the Russians would make a powerful ally – whether to Britain and her allies, or to Nazi Germany and hers; there was also the worry that the Soviet Union might devour Poland and other countries, whether she made an alliance with Germany or with Britain. However, he told the Poles that *'from the moment when the Nazi malignity is plain, a definite association between Poland and Russia becomes indispensable'*.

Churchill had always been deeply suspicious of Socialists, let alone Communists. In a 1920 article for the *Illustrated Sunday Herald*, he described Communism as *'a pestilence more destructive of life than the Black Death or the Spotted Typhus'*; on another occasion he remarked, *'Trying to maintain good relations with a Communist is like wooing a crocodile. You do not know whether to tickle it under the chin or beat it over the head. When it opens its mouth, you cannot tell whether it is trying to smile or preparing to eat you up.'*

Of the comparatively new Soviet Union he remarked in 1919: *'Here we have a state whose subjects are so happy that they have to be forbidden to quit its bounds under the direst penalties; whose diplomatists and agents sent on foreign missions have often to leave their wives and children at home to ensure their eventual return.'* He also said, *'In Russia a man is called reactionary if he objects to having his property stolen, and his wife and children murdered.'*

And: *'There is not one single social or economic principle or concept in the philosophy of the Russian Bolshevik which has not been realized, carried into action, and enshrined in immutable laws a million years ago by the white ant.'*

It was not, however, the time to be picky about one's allies. In the spring of 1939, Churchill met the Soviet Ambassador Ivan Maisky. *'Now look here, Mr Ambassador,'* the conversation (one-sided, apparently) is supposed to have gone, *'if we are to make a success of this new policy, we require the help of Russia. Now I don't care for your system and I never have, but the Poles and Romanians like it even less. Although they might be prepared at a pinch to let you in, they would certainly want some assurances that you would eventually get out.'*

Lloyd George expressed his disapproval of the idea of an alliance with the Soviets, to be airily – and somewhat cryptically – dismissed by Churchill: *'You must not do this sort of thing, my dear. You are putting spokes in the wheel of history.'*

In June, Churchill called for the creation of a Triple Alliance between Britain, France and Russia – but in spite of his disappointment in Hitler's behaviour, Chamberlain still hoped to appease the German Chancellor – and knew that paying attention to

Churchill would certainly not do that. Neither, of course, would appointing Churchill to the Cabinet, as some were calling for. According to the editor of the *Sunday Pictorial*, his readers overwhelmingly wanted a strong man in the government who would stop the 'boot-licking to Hitler', while the *Observer* more moderately pointed out, 'That one who has so firm a grasp of the realities of European politics should not be included in the Government must be as bewildering to foreigners as it is regrettable to most of his countrymen.'

'Chamberlain's obstinate exclusion of Churchill from the Cabinet is taken as a sign that he has not abandoned appeasement and that all gesture of resistance is mere bluff,' Harold Nicolson wrote in his diary. General William Ironside, in 1938 Governor of Gibraltar, noted, 'He is a pacifist at heart. He has a firm belief that God has chosen him as an instrument to prevent this threatened war. He can never get this out of his mind. He is not against Winston, but he believes that chances may still arrive for averting war, and he thinks that Winston might be so strong in a Cabinet that he would be prevented from acting.'

In the meantime a collection of Churchill's newspaper articles was published under the title *Step by Step*. 'It must be a melancholy satisfaction to see how right you were,' Clement Attlee remarked to him. Churchill – for once – kept out of the arguments. He was busy working, with the help of the historians Bill Deakin and Alan Bullock, on his *History of the English-Speaking Peoples*: *'It is a relief in times like these to be able to escape into other centuries.'*

In August, the holiday period (and Chamberlain had adjourned Parliament), Churchill – perhaps seeking support for Britain and her allies further afield – spoke to the American nation:

> *How did we spend our summer holidays twenty-five years ago?* . . . *Why, those were the days when Prussian militarism was – to quote its own phrase – 'hacking its way through the small weak neighbour country' whose neutrality and independence they had sworn not merely to respect but to defend.*

He himself had a short holiday in France, where he did a spot of painting – *'This,'* he said sadly, turning to a painter friend, Paul Maze, who was sitting painting nearby, *'is the last picture we shall paint in peace for a very long time.'* He returned to Britain to hear that Germany and the Soviet Union had made a non-aggression pact.

Soon after, on 1 September, Germany invaded Poland. Chamberlain still hoped for peace but decided to form a War Cabinet, which he invited Churchill to join. The next two days the Prime Minister and Lord Halifax spent trying to persuade Hitler to pull back – to no avail, an ultimatum was ignored, and at last, on the Sunday, at 11.15 in the morning, Chamberlain broadcast that Britain was at war with Germany.

Churchill was invited to join the Cabinet as First Lord of the Admiralty, and the signal was sent to all Royal Navy vessels and bases: 'Winston is Back!'

Lord Mountbatten recalled the day in a speech to the Churchill Centre. He had just been given command of a fleet of destroyers, which were 'a lovely light grey' – with the imminent prospect of war they had to be painted a darker colour and he was himself hanging over the side with a paintbrush when his chief yeoman of signals came along and said, 'War, sir, war telegram. Commence hostilities against Germany.' Ten minutes later, as Mountbatten was digesting this news miserably, the chief yeoman came back. 'He was waving a telegram and saying: "Telegram from the Admiralty, sir. Winston is back." Just that – "Winston is back". It had an electric effect throughout the Fleet. Everyone said: "Now, we are going to go places."'

Chapter 9

First Lord Again

CHURCHILL GOT BUSY. True to form, he found it imperative that he should involve himself in everything that was going on. And where the Royal Navy was concerned, he did not hold back in his interfering – Winston was definitely back.

Sir Samuel Hoare wrote to Lord Beaverbrook on 1 October, describing what it was like having Churchill back: 'Winston has been much as you expected he would be, very rhetorical, emotional and, most of all, very reminiscent. He strikes me as an old man who easily gets tired.' This might have been malicious – he had no reason to love Churchill – but he did go on to say, 'I should say that at the moment he is the one popular figure in the Cabinet.' As for getting tired, it is less likely to have been due to his age than to have been due to the amount of work he got through every day: letters and memorandums, meetings and conferences, speeches to compose and dictate, books to write . . . According to a junior Admiralty minister, Geoffrey Shakespeare, quoted in *The Churchill War Papers*, he held a naval conference every night after dinner, 'But after 11 p.m. he devoted himself to speech making . . . One night he remarked, *"Are you all ready? I'm feeling very fertile tonight."'* Although Churchill himself remarked that he would have to strive his utmost *'to keep pace with the genera-tion now in power',* most people were astonished at his energy, Violet Bonham Carter writing to him, 'You need no blood transfusions, unlike some of your colleagues.' He had the effect of a whirlwind. Chips (Sir Henry) Channon wrote in his diary, 'I am told that Winston is already driving the Admiralty to distraction by his inter-ference and energy.' To Kathleen Hill, Churchill's secretary, the Admiralty when Churchill was away 'was dead, dead, dead'. When he was there 'the place was buzzing with atmosphere, with electricity'.

He took an observant and fresh interest in naval matters. It is said that when inspecting the harbour at Scapa Flow, he astonished the officer taking him round by immediately spotting the dummy fishing vessel hiding the naval fleet. 'But, sir,' said the officer, 'she's not even been spotted by our own reconnaissance!'

'Then they need spectacles.'

'How so, sir?'

'No gulls.'

There are always scavenging seagulls flocking around fishing vessels. Churchill recommended that they should attract the gulls with food: *'Feed the gulls and fool the Germans.'* They followed his advice.

By now an inveterate scribbler, Churchill wrote memorandums copiously, sent minutes around the department, annotated other memos and minutes before sending them off on their journeys round the Admiralty and to some senior naval officers. For these annotations he used either a red or a green pen – *'Must have port and starboard,'* he explained to a bystander. It was probably with one of these that he scribbled on a report from his naval adviser Admiral Dudley Pound, the words *'Penny foolish'*.

As many of his memos ended with requests such as *'Pray inform me'* or *'Pray send me',* they soon became known round the Admiralty as the 'First Lord's Prayers'. There were some who found his many communications a bit excessive: 'All your letters are carefully read and considered by me,' wrote Chamberlain, who must have been feeling his grip on the premiership slip, 'and if I have not replied to them, it is only because I am seeing you every day, and moreover, because as far as I have been able to observe, your views and mine have very closely coincided.'

Churchill set high store by the written word, and believed that everybody should read memos and other communications thoroughly – as he himself did. An additional advantage for him was his eidetic memory, which meant that he always remembered what he read or saw. In *Assignment to Catastrophe*, General Spears recollected that Clementine Churchill advised him to 'put what you have to say in writing. He often does not listen or does not hear if he is thinking of something else. But he will always consider a paper carefully and take in all its implications. He never forgets what he sees in writing.'

Chamberlain's confidence in the security of his job cannot have been boosted by Roosevelt's choice of pen pal. On 4 September, only the day after Churchill's appointment as First Lord, the President of the United States wrote to him. 'What I want you and the Prime Minister to know,' asserted Roosevelt, 'is that I shall at all times welcome it if you will keep me in touch personally with anything you want me to know about.' With Chamberlain's blessing, this developed into a regular, and very important correspondence – and a vital alliance.

> An elderly statesman with gout,
> When asked what the war was about,
> In a Written Reply
> Said, 'My colleagues and I
> Are doing our best to find out.'

Who composed this limerick about Chamberlain, which began to go round the House of Parliament, is not known, but it had more than an element of truth – to which might be added that the elderly statesman did not know what to do about the war, either.

War on Germany having been declared, there came a pause while Britain decided what to do (and Churchill sent memos round). The RAF was prepared to drop bombs when so instructed, but the Luftwaffe were by now much feared and most of the British army was scattered in the Middle East and India, with the British Expeditionary Force in north-eastern France. That left the Royal Navy, for which the First Lord came up with many plans. He had reckoned without the German navy, though, and an aircraft carrier, *Courageous* and the battleship *Royal Oak* were sunk early on, but the year ended on a more cheerful note (for the Allies) when the German ship *Admiral Graf Spee*, was sunk off Montevideo in South America.

For some months – during which time the Soviet Union invaded eastern Poland (on 17 September) and Finland (on 30 November) – the Cabinet and Chiefs of

Staff discussed Churchill's schemes to take control of the waters off neutral Norway and halt German sea traffic's passage and block access to Norwegian and Swedish iron ore, essential to Germany's war industry.

Churchill was scathing about countries that remained neutral in the belief that this would protect them from the Nazis: while Finland fought gallantly against the massive Soviet Union in a war that lasted until March the following year, Norway, Sweden and Denmark, Switzerland, the Netherlands and Belgium all kept quiet before the marching Germans – *'Each one hopes that if he feeds the crocodile enough,'* commented Churchill, *'the crocodile will eat him last.'* In the event, all the countries were overrun except for Switzerland in its mountain stronghold, with its banks.

Britain's eventual plan was to mine the sea and have forces ready to take control of Norwegian ports as and when necessary to hold the Germans back. Hitler, however, had had a simpler plan, and one that would be more quickly executed: to take Norway and Denmark. General Nikolaus von Falkenhorst later recalled a meeting he had with Hitler on 20 February. 'He [Hitler] led me to a table covered with maps. "I have a similar thing in mind," he said. "The occupation of Norway; because I am informed that the English intend to land there, and I want to be there before them."'

The Royal Navy laid their mines on 8 April. By the end of the following day German troops had taken their primary objectives (with the aid of the Norwegian National Union Party, whose leader Vidkun Quisling was made head of a puppet Norwegian government). Had the Royal Navy been better prepared for this – and this has a familiar ring to it – the war might have been

shorter. As it is, the German navy was virtually put out of
action for some months, but British losses (and French
and Polish) were also heavy.

On 26 April, the *New York Post* contained 'the first
and only eyewitness report on the opening chapter of
the British expeditionary troops' advance in Norway
north of Trondheim':

> It is a bitterly disillusioning and almost unbelievable
> story.
>
> The British force which was supposed to sweep down
> from Namsos consisted of one battalion of Territorials
> and one battalion of the King's Own Royal Light
> Infantry. These totalled fewer than 1,500 men. They
> were dumped into Norway's deep snows and quagmires
> of April slush without a single anti-aircraft gun, without
> one squadron of supporting airplanes, without a single
> piece of field artillery.
>
> They were thrown into the snows and mud of 63
> degrees north latitude to fight crack German regulars –
> most of them veterans of the Polish invasion – and to
> face the most destructive of modern weapons. The great
> majority of these young Britishers averaged only one
> year of military service. They have already paid a heavy
> price for a major military blunder which was not
> committed by their immediate command, but in
> London.
>
> Unless they receive large supplies of anti-air guns and
> adequate reinforcements within a very few days, the
> remains of these two British battalions will be cut to
> ribbons.
>
> Here is the astonishing story of what has happened to
> the gallant little handful of British expeditionaries above

Trondheim: After only four days of fighting, nearly half of this initial BEF contingent has been knocked out – either killed, wounded or captured. On Monday, these comparatively inexperienced and incredibly under-armed British troops were decisively defeated. They were driven back in precipitate disorder from Vist, three miles south of the bomb-ravaged town of Steinkjer.

By the end of May, British troops had been withdrawn from all of Norway except the port of Narvik, which they evacuated on 8 June, abandoning Norway to her fate.

There is a tale that, following the British withdrawal from Norway, it was proposed that, for their next foray into Norway, the Royal Marines should all have sheaths to protect the ten-and-a-half-inch barrels of their rifles from the sharp temperature changes. A pharmaceutical company that specialized in manufacturing condoms was given the job. In due course the first box was delivered to Churchill for his inspection. He looked at the box and muttered, *'Won't do.'* He drew a carton out of the box, shook his head and muttered *'Won't do'* again. He opened the carton and took out a packet. *'Won't do.'*

'What do you mean it won't do?' an aide asked him. 'They are long enough for the barrels – ten and a half inches.'

'Labels,' came the cryptic reply.

'Labels?'

'Yes. I want a label for every box, every carton, every packet, saying "British. Size: Medium". That will show the Nazis, if they ever recover one of them, who's the master race.'

*

The loss of Norway was indeed a sorry tale – and the responsibility lay, as on an earlier occasion, with the First Lord of the Admiralty. This time, however, the outcome was different. Outweighing the Norway disaster was the general perception that Churchill had been right all the time, during his ten years of bombarding everyone with warnings about Germany's military strength, and Hitler's military and political intentions. As Clementine later remarked to him, it was only his long-standing opposition to Hitler that saved him from being blamed for Norway. Moreover, as First Lord of the Admiralty, Churchill was the only minister who had any kind of dramatic news to broadcast to the public, and he found it expedient (to keep up morale) to exaggerate the Royal Navy's accomplishments, and to dwell triumphantly on the sinking of German U-boats. (One evening as early as October 1939, when the Churchills were dining at the Chamberlains', news arrived of the sinking of a U-boat (first course?), then, again, of the sinking of another (second course?); then for pudding, another U-boat was apparently sunk. Had it all been arranged on purpose? enquired Mrs Chamberlain – but they went to bed happy. In the morning the news was of the sinking of the *Royal Oak*, but there was no mention of U-boats.)

And Churchill could not be held responsible for the delay in acting – had the Allies blockaded the Norwegian waters when he first mooted the scheme, they might have met with greater success, but by April, with the melting of useful natural blockades in the form of ice, the Allies lost an advantage. '*Victory will never be found by taking the line of least resistance,*' Churchill had written to Halifax in January. And in March: '*Now the ice will melt; and the Germans are the masters of the North.'*

In France as in Britain, the politicians tended to drag their heels unlike the military (and Churchill), who saw how dangerous delay was. *'Nous allons perdre l'omnibus,'* Churchill told General Alphonse Georges.

The parliamentary debate on Norway was lively. 'Norway followed Czechoslovakia and Poland. Everywhere the story is "too late",' Attlee pointed out, laying the blame at the feet of the government, rather than on Churchill. Amery was even more direct and, addressing Chamberlain, quoted Cromwell's dismissal of the Long Parliament – 'You have sat too long here for any good you have been doing. Depart, I say, and let us have done with you. In the name of God, go.' Lloyd George reminded the Prime Minister that he had met Hitler in peace and in war and had always been worsted.

> He has appealed for sacrifice. The nation is prepared for every sacrifice so long as it has leadership . . . I say solemnly that the Prime Minister should give an example of sacrifice because there is nothing which can contribute more to victory in this war than that he should sacrifice the seals of office.

As Lloyd George spoke up for Churchill, Churchill stood up to declare that he took full responsibility for everything the Admiralty had done and that he was taking his *'full share of the burden'*. To this gallant attempt to protect the Prime Minister and others, Lloyd George responded: 'The right honourable gentleman must not allow himself to be converted into an air-raid shelter to keep the splinters from hitting his colleagues.'

The debate went on for a very long time, becoming very rowdy, and ended with a majority vote in favour of Chamberlain, who nevertheless saw that it was time to go. Halifax was offered the job, which he declined (his peerage disqualified him, he said, and the thought 'left me with a bad stomach ache'); this was probably as well: after his visit to Nazi Germany four years before, according to Chips Channon, 'He told me he liked all the Nazi leaders, even Goebbels, and he was much impressed, interested and amused by the visit. He thinks the regime absolutely fantastic.' He had undoubtedly changed his mind since, as had Chamberlain, but, had he become Prime Minister, a public revelation of this nature would have been disastrous. Nevertheless his tendencies still leaned towards appeasement. Churchill once remarked: *'Halifax's virtues have done more harm than the vices of hundreds of other people.'*

There was only one other politician of any stature, and that was Winston Churchill. The Cabinet was by no means unanimously in favour of him – but then, early in the morning of 10 May, just as Churchill had predicted, Nazi forces flooded into the Netherlands, Belgium and Luxembourg, bringing the Phoney War to an end.

Chamberlain went to Buckingham Palace to see the King, who, disappointed that Halifax had turned down the premiership, asked him his advice, 'and he told me Winston was the man to send for'.

The moment Churchill had been waiting for had arrived. *'I felt as if I were walking with Destiny, and that all my past life had been but a preparation for this hour and for this trial,'* he concluded *The Gathering Storm*, first volume of *The Second World War. 'I thought I knew a good deal about it all, and I was sure I should not fail.'*

Chapter 10

Good Old Winnie

'*I* *have nothing to offer but blood, toil, tears and sweat,*' Winston Churchill famously announced in Parliament on 13 May 1940, his first address as Prime Minister (the phrase adapted from poems by John Donne and by Byron, testament to the breadth of both Churchill's reading and his memory). '*Victory at all costs, victory in spite of all terror, victory however long and hard the road may be; for without victory there is no survival.*'

His audience was electrified. As he walked out of the Chamber he turned to his friend Desmond Morton: 'That *got the sods, didn't it!*'

Paul Joseph Goebbels, Hitler's minister of propaganda, and therefore well qualified to recognize a good bit of PR, commented, 'His slogan of "blood, sweat and tears" has entrenched him in a position that makes him totally immune from attack. He's like the doctor who prophesies that his patient will die and who, every time his patient's condition worsens, smugly explains that he prophesied it.'

Churchill now had the task of forming his coalition War Cabinet. He gave a number of leading Labour politicians – Clement Attlee, Ernest Bevin, Herbert Morrison, Stafford Cripps and Hugh Dalton – key positions, and he made Anthony Eden Secretary of State for War (later that year Eden replaced Lord Halifax as Foreign Secretary, and Halifax, not entirely trusted, was sent to Washington as Ambassador).

'*I displayed the smiling confidence and confident air which are thought suitable when things are very bad,*' Churchill later wrote in *Their Finest Hour*, the second volume of *The Second World War*. At the time, recognizing what a huge task he had ahead of him, he said to General Hastings Ismay, on the Imperial Defence Committee, of the British people who had welcomed his appointment rather more warmly than had some of his colleagues, '*Poor people, poor people. They trust me, and I can give them nothing but disaster for quite a long time.*'

The '*old turnip*', Stanley Baldwin, wrote to him, 'From the bottom of my heart I wish you all that is good – health and strength of mind and body – for the intolerable burden that now lies on you.' Churchill was to write to Baldwin during the difficult war years, '*I cannot say that I am enjoying being Prime Minister very much.*'

He continued to work unceasingly – and to meddle like mad (had it been current in his day he would probably have approved of the term 'hands-on approach'). He now had more to interfere with. He continued with quaint politeness to request action and information.

'I knew some people in Naval Intelligence,' Alistair Cooke recalled in a talk at a conference of the International Churchill Societies. 'I remember one man who I don't think got over it for years. He said, "We were all in our thirties, late thirties. We'd get to sleep at midnight, and at quarter to three in the morning the telephone would ring. It was the Prime Minister. He would say, *'Pray, discover and draft for me the soundings in the bay of Rio de Janeiro.'* So we'd stay up all night working on these tasks, which we called 'the Prime Minister's prayers'. Every other night we'd start work at three o'clock in the morning.'"

Churchill shuttled to and from France, accompanied by Hastings ('Pug') Ismay, to try to bolster up French morale and resistance, and persuade them to attack German supply lines by floating mines down the Rhine. The French premier, Paul Reynaud, kept on changing his mind; Ismay suggested to Churchill that Madame de Portes, Reynaud's mistress, had considerable – and decisive – influence over him. *'We* must *face up to it, Pug,'* replied Churchill, *'she has certain advantages that we have not.'*

Things *were* very bad. On 12 May, two days after they had invaded the Low Countries, the German forces entered France. On the 15th the Netherlands capitulated. The German war machine, with massed tanks and Stuka dive-bombers, made its inexorable way across France. It reached Abbeville, on the French coast, by the 20th, no more than a week after its original penetration into France, and in so doing split the Allied forces in two, French and British armies to the north, French armies to the south. It seemed just a matter of time before this lethal combination of aircraft, armour and infantry – Blitzkrieg – made its way across the Channel and invaded Britain. In the meanwhile, there were the British forces in France to think about. By the beginning of June over 335,000 Allied soldiers had been evacuated from Dunkirk, in 'Operation Dynamo' – *'out*

*of the jaws of death and shame, to their native land and
to the tasks which lie immediately ahead.'*

Churchill gave one of his most famous rallying
speeches, on 4 June:

> *We shall not flag or fail. We shall go on to the end. We
> shall fight in France, we shall fight on the seas and
> oceans, we shall fight with growing confidence and
> growing strength in the air, we shall defend our island,
> whatever the cost may be, we shall fight on the beaches,
> we shall fight on the landing grounds, we shall fight in
> the fields and in the streets, we shall fight in the hills; we
> shall never surrender.*

Pausing in the great uproar that greeted these words,
Churchill muttered to a colleague next to him, *'And
we'll fight them with the butt ends of broken beer bottles
because that's bloody well all we've got!'*

In the United States – neutral at the time – President
Roosevelt heard the speech in a radio broadcast and
commented to his aide, Harry Hopkins, 'As long as that
old bastard is in charge, Britain will never surrender.'

Years later Clement Attlee was asked exactly what
Churchill did to win the war. He replied: 'Talk about it.'
He did not mean only the Prime Minister's public
speeches and broadcasts, and his discussions with
politicians at home and abroad – he meant all the time.
Churchill talked non-stop, in private as well as in public,
to whatever audience presented itself – including his
pets. To Jock Colville's surprise he talked exclusively to
his marmalade cat through an entire lunchtime.

On 10 June Italy declared war on the Allies, and on
the 14th Paris fell; as Hitler prepared to accept the
French surrender from the new French premier,

Marshal Henri Pétain (a hero of the First World War, who, an old man now, believed that capitulation was the best thing for the French people, given the position the country was in. He was later condemned as a traitor, but, given his age, the death sentence was commuted to life imprisonment on an island, where he died, aged ninety, in 1951.) *'I grieve for the gallant French people,'* said Churchill. *'What has happened in France makes no difference to our actions and purpose.'* Following France's capitulation, on the 22nd, Churchill, with regret, ordered the destruction of her fleet, to keep it from falling into German hands.

On 18 June, Churchill sent out his famous call to arms – with a clear message to the US President:

> . . . *If we can stand up to him* [Hitler], *all Europe may be free . . . But if we fail, then the whole world, including the United States . . . will sink into the abyss of a new dark age . . . Let us therefore brace ourselves to our duty and so bear ourselves that if the British Empire and its Commonwealth lasts for a thousand years men will still say, 'This was their finest hour.'*

The country prepared to meet a German invasion. Across the Channel the Germans were massing transport vessels and landing craft ready to invade – in 'Operation Sealion'.

Randolph Churchill many years later told his son Winston how he went to see his father in Downing Street one morning that summer. He found the Prime Minister standing before a shaving mirror, naked apart from a short silk vest, which was the only thing he would wear to sleep in. Randolph seated himself on the end of the bed, intently watching the reflection of his father's face in the shaving mirror. For some considerable time, the latter remained silent. Then suddenly, fixing him with his eye in the mirror, he declared: '*I think I see my way through: we shall have to drag in the Americans.*'

He never did 'drag in' the Americans – they came into the war the following year, when Hitler declared war on them, after they had declared war on Japan in response to the bombing of Pearl Harbor. Neither did the Germans invade Britain. The planned invasion was temporarily postponed until Britain's air force could be destroyed. Instead came the Battle of Britain as, on 10 July, the Germans launched the might of the Luftwaffe (so much greater than the RAF's) from air bases established across the Channel, with the aim of winning command of the skies over Britain by destroying Fighter Command, and by bombing, then annihilating British naval and airborne defences, before setting 'Operation Sealion' into motion.

'Churchill has said that he will fight on . . . now I realize the continuation of this war means the destruction of one or the other of the adversaries,' Hitler declared on 19 July. 'Churchill thinks it's going to be Germany. But I think it's going to be Britain.'

The RAF's Fighter Command was seriously outnumbered by the Luftwaffe – by about four to one – but had certain advantages, notably in that their two main fighters were exceptional aircraft, as good as or better than anything the Germans had, and they had shorter lines of communications. As well as this, the C-in-C Fighter Command, Air Chief Marshal Sir Hugh Dowding, had had an early request granted for a chain of early-warning radar stations, which enabled them to ready themselves for whatever incoming aircraft were on their way. On 15 August the RAF shot down seventy-six German aircraft with a loss of thirty-four of its own fighters. A few days later came Churchill's famous tribute: *'Never in the field of human conflict was so much owed by so many to so few.'*

His friend Violet Bonham Carter wrote to him rapturously to say that she believed that sentence 'will live as long as words are spoken and remembered. Nothing so simple, so majestic and so true has been said in so great a moment of human history. You have beaten your old enemies "the Classics" into a cocked hat!'

One of the RAF fighter pilots, Hugh Dundas, remarked how when they heard his words, 'We all puffed our chests out a bit and thought how important we were, but until then, I don't think we thought about it particularly.'

It is likely, however, that the RAF might have been defeated had it not been for the Germans' accidental bombing of London – which led to the British bombing Berlin in reprisal. At that point the German forces turned their attention to London, killing some 45,000 British civilians in the Blitz, which lasted from 7 September 1940 until the following May, coming to a close at about the same time as Churchill came to the end of his first year as Prime Minister. During the course of the Blitz, according to a speech he made to the Commons in 1942, Churchill added to his original programme of *'blood, toil, tears, and sweat'*, *'many shortcomings, mistakes and disappointments'.*

It was, to say the least, an eventful war – but at least no major difficulties were put in his way by his government. As Clement Attlee, Labour Party leader and Lord Privy

Seal (until 1942), wrote in his memoir, *As It Happened* (1954):

> We were all united in the great task of ensuring our national survival. Labour and Conservative Members worked wholeheartedly together and differences on Party lines did not arise. There was also unity between military and civilians . . . We had a Prime Minister who understood war and a high proportion of Ministers had served in the First World War, and this made for greater understanding.

Among the military, those closest to him, the Chiefs of Staff, included Ismay (Chief of Staff to the Minister of Defence – Churchill himself), General Sir Alan Brooke (Chief of the Imperial General Staff from 1941), Air Chief Marshal Sir Charles Portal, and Admiral Sir Dudley Pound, First Sea Lord until October 1943, when he was succeeded by Admiral Sir Andrew Cunningham. They were a formidable group – and unsurprisingly quite often found the Prime Minister a nightmare to deal with as he took over, or tried to take over, their commands when it suited him. Fortunately he had had the foresight to place as a kind of 'manager', or middleman, of the Chiefs of Staff Committee, his friend Pug Ismay. This appointment, Ismay recalled in his *Memoirs*,

> . . . gave rise to not a little suspicion and resentment. My duties were never specifically defined, and it was left to me to interpret them as best I could. First and foremost I made it my business to express, and if necessary to explain, Churchill's views to the Chiefs of Staff Committee, and to inform him of their reactions. Now and then a certain amount of tactful expurgation was

necessary . . . I had to be not only an interpreter, but a mediator.

Churchill's encounters, verbal and otherwise, with the members of his Chiefs of Staff Committee and with many other senior military and naval figures, would fill many a book, especially given the differing versions of the many stories. But rarely is there no hint of affection.

He was, for instance, fond of the elderly First Sea Lord, Admiral Pound (just what did he mean by *'penny foolish'* – that Pound was wise, perhaps?). *'Dudley Pound is a funny old boy,'* Churchill, as First Lord of the Admiralty for the second time, once remarked to a colleague. *'People think he's always asleep, but you've only got to suggest reducing the naval estimates by a million and he's awake in a flash.'*

One night in 1940 Pound was taking part in an after-dinner discussion with Churchill and Generals Wavell (C-in-C Middle East) and Dill (Chief of Imperial General Staff) when there was an air-raid warning, as Jock Colville, who was also there, relates. They made their way out into the dark garden, but Pound was rather lame and fell down a flight of steps. He picked himself up and fell down some more steps to land in a heap near a sentry who, thinking him an intruder, ran up to him with his bayonet at the ready. 'This is not the place for a First Sea Lord,' said the First Sea Lord sadly, as the other members of the party ran up to help him. Churchill gazed down at him fondly. *'Try to remember that you are an Admiral of the Fleet and not a midshipman,'* he said.

Pound might also be the subject of the *'Rum, sodomy and lash'* story – if it is not apocryphal. According to the story Churchill had suggested to an admiral (possibly Pound) the provision of better conditions for ordinary seamen – to be told that this would be 'against the traditions' of the Royal Navy. Churchill is said to have retorted: *'Traditions! What traditions? Rum, sodomy – and the lash!'* Anthony Montague Browne said of the phrase that Churchill 'liked it very much, but he had never heard it before' – but this was when Churchill was an old man and perhaps he had forgotten the occasion. Jock Colville, another of his Private Secretaries, on the other hand, seems to think that Churchill did utter those words – to Sir Dudley Pound, adding that 'Pound had a slow, wry sense of humour, but this was going too far.'

General Sir Alan Brooke (C-in-C Home Forces, from July 1940 to December 1941, when Churchill appointed him CIGS; later to be Field Marshal Lord Alanbrooke) was less tolerant of his meddling Prime Minister, on one occasion spluttering furiously into his diary, 'He knows no details, has only got half the picture in his mind, talks absurdities and makes my blood boil to listen to his nonsense . . . And the wonderful thing is that ¾ of the population of the world imagine Winston Churchill is one of the great Strategists of History, a second Marlborough, and the other ¼ have no conception of what a public menace he is.'

But he also said, 'Winston is a marvel. I can't imagine how he sticks it'; 'He is quite the most wonderful man I have ever met, and is a source of never-ending interest to me'; and 'He is the most difficult man I have ever served, but thank God for having given me the opportunity'.

Churchill found that *'Brookie'* stood up to him, which, in fact, he liked: *'When I thump the table and push my face towards him, what does he do?'* he said. *'Thumps the table harder and glares back at me.'* He was, however, deeply hurt by Alanbrooke's diaries, which were published shortly after the war.

One of Churchill's secretaries, Elizabeth Nel, told of how one day, Churchill was in the bedroom, in the middle of a most serious telephone conversation with General Alan Brooke, when his little Persian cat Smokey bit his toes. As he kicked the cat off, Churchill exclaimed, *'Get off, you fool!'* – which the bewildered general took to be addressed to himself.

One of Churchill's favourite military men was Field Marshal Sir Harold Alexander – *'He is no glory-hopper'* – but another favourite field marshal, Bernard Law Montgomery, was a greater source of amusement to him, with his self-righteousness ('I neither drink nor smoke and am a hundred per cent fit'), his lack of humour and his self-regard, on top of his good qualities (*'This vehement and formidable general . . . austere, severe, accomplished, tireless,'* Churchill wrote of him). It is related that just before the Battle of El Alamein, having decided that General Montgomery should take command of the Eighth Army in North Africa, he summoned the General to London. *'I think,'* said Churchill, always full of advice, *'that you would be well advised to study the science that Americans call logistics. That is to say, the correct disposition of your ships and lorry trains, so that your men in the front lines may get everything they need.'*

'I am sure you are right, sir,' replied Montgomery, 'but I am wondering if I should become personally involved in such purely technical matters, because, after all, you know they say familiarity breeds contempt.'

'I perceive your point, General,' countered Churchill. *'But I would like to remind you that without a degree of familiarity, nothing could breed!'*

Later, during the El Alamein battle, the Eighth Army captured the temporary commanding officer of the Afrika Korps, General Wilhelm von Thoma. Montgomery decided to invite his German counterpart, prisoner or not, to dine with him in his GHQ trailer. Some were scandalized, though not the Prime Minister: *'I sympathize with General von Thoma. Defeated, humiliated, in captivity, and . . .* dinner with General Montgomery.'

'In retreat indomitable; in advance invincible; in victory insufferable' is how Churchill described Montgomery (a variation of his epigraph: *'In war: resolution; In defeat: defiance; In victory: magnanimity; In peace: goodwill'* – said to have originally been offered, at the end of the First World War, to a French town as a memorial; the lines, however, were politely declined – apparently on the grounds that the shattered citizens found the idea of magnanimity and goodwill too hard to take). He is also said to have used a similar phrase of Montgomery – *'In defeat, unbeatable; in victory, unbearable.'*

Churchill was fond of Montgomery, though, and Monty remained a faithful friend to the end, visiting him at Chartwell – not necessarily by invitation – where the two old men sat together and exchanged reminiscences over tea.

In his book, *The Churchillians*, Jock Colville recalled how the Prime Minister was sometimes impatient with the Chiefs of Staff, usually because he felt they were being over-cautious. General Ismay, he said, reported

that the Prime Minister left a meeting of the Defence
Committee with the parting shot: *'I am expected to wage
modern war with antiquated weapons.'* In March 1941,
during the Greek campaign, Colville went into the
Prime Minister's bedroom, when he was due to wake up
from his afternoon siesta, with an urgent message.
Churchill woke up to remark, *'The poor Chiefs of Staff
will get very much out of breath in their desire to run
away.'*

Inevitably, there were tensions and, in private,
outbursts of temper on the part of the Prime Minister
were not infrequent. On 28 May 1940 he sent a memo
round his colleagues: *'In these dark days the Prime
Minister would be grateful if all his colleagues . . . would
maintain a high morale in their circles . . .'* He himself
found it difficult to maintain the appearance of high
morale – a letter of reproof came from Clementine a
couple of months later: '. . . there is a danger of your
being generally disliked by your colleagues and
subordinates because of your rough sarcastic and
overbearing manner . . .'

Even poor Rufus the poodle didn't escape his wrath
(though a self-deprecatory hint of humour was not far
behind) when an outburst of Churchill's set him
barking. Churchill turned to his secretary – *'Take that
dog away! We cannot both be barking at once.'* He was
usually quick to soften and become conciliatory.

On an occasion when he was angry with Colville for
some reason and summoned him to take dictation at
some very anti-social hour, Colville protested that he
didn't know shorthand – it's brief, take it down in
longhand, he was told sharply. Which he did. Suddenly
seeking to appease, Churchill then proceeded to

compliment Colville fulsomely on his handwriting, somewhat to the latter's surprise.

And when one of his bodyguards, Inspector Davis, fussed over him when he had fallen in the pond while feeding his swans, he snapped at him, *'Shut your bloody mouth.'* As they entered the house, however, he turned and put his arm across Davis's shoulders: *'You know, Davis, your mouth isn't really bloody.'*

On another occasion during the war, Inspector Thompson recollected, as he walked with Churchill towards Downing Street, a young boy came walking along in the opposite direction whistling cheerfully. *'Stop that whistling,'* Churchill demanded. 'Why should I?' *'Because I don't like it, and it's a horrible noise.'* 'Well, you can shut your ears, can't you?' And the boy strolled off unconcerned. Churchill was astounded and furious. Then he began to smile, repeating the words *'You can shut your ears, can't you?'* and chuckling.

As he said to Ismay, *'Pug, this is a world of vice and woe – of vice and woe. But I'll take the vice and you can have the woe!'*

During the Blitz Churchill came to see the PR value of showing himself in the streets. He was instantly recognizable – by his accoutrements if nothing else; to his striped trousers and spotted bow tie, were always added a cigar, a walking stick, a hat (of which he had a number, all distinctive). As he walked through the crowds he always acknowledged people's greetings with the V-sign. (This worried some of his aides at first, who thought it was vulgar – and that it might be misinterpreted.) Then, of course, there was the famous siren suit.

*

Churchill liked dressing up – a trait in keeping with his self-dramatization – and quite often wore one or another fancy uniform. Clementine Churchill told Anthony Montague Browne how he once, in 1918, amazed the French premier Georges Clemenceau (the 'old tiger', Churchill's favourite Frenchman) when he wore his uniform of Elder Brother of Trinity House (an organization responsible for lighthouses and other marine markers) to a reception prior to going on to a Trinity House dinner. Why, Clemenceau asked him, are you dressed as a semi-naval officer. *'Je suis,'* Churchill explained impressively, *'un Frère Aîné de la Trinité.'* 'Ah. Quelle belle situation,' remarked Clemenceau.

He had a number of other uniforms – military and quasi-military – which he wore as and when appropriate or when the fancy took him. On one occasion, his valet Norman McGowan recalled, he was wearing his uniform of Lord Warden of the Cinque Ports during a tour of duty when one of his epaulettes fell off. He continued unperturbed, but when he got home he remarked to McGowan, *'It's a good job I personally fasten my braces.'*

Mr Barry Reed had just joined the renowned family firm of Austin Reed (which had made the uniform) at the time and remembered the consternation the minor mishap caused – no one, he said lost their job, but it was a near-run thing.

Churchill was particularly fond of his 'siren suits', which were also made for him by Austin Reed, and would certainly have been more comfortable than his various uniforms and his pin-striped suits. His bodyguard Edmund Murray described it as being like 'a glamorized boiler suit, really, made in one piece more or less, with a zip fastener down the front'. Occasionally when waiting for Churchill, Murray would hear a roar, and would know that he had zipped himself up with too much zeal.

The siren suit was not just for wearing when the air-raid sirens sounded, or to lure sailors on to rocks. He quite often wore one round the house. He was wearing one the day Murray first arrived at Chartwell to start his new job in August 1950, with a silver-grey Stetson hat on his head and on his feet royal-blue velvet bedroom slippers with the initials WSC embroidered in gold thread. A dazzling sight he must have presented. He also wore one, rather more bizarrely, when visiting the troops in the Western Desert (with an Australian bush-hat on his head), and he was even photographed in Washington, DC, clad in his siren suit.

Ismay described one of Churchill's visits to the bombed docks area of London in September 1940 (though he did not say what Churchill was wearing): '"Good old Winnie," they cried. "We thought you'd come and see us. We can take it. Give it 'em back." Churchill broke down, and as I was struggling to get him through the crowd, I heard an old woman say, "You see, he really cares. He's crying."'

He did care – but it was he, too, who had told them that they could take it. That things were going to be terrible but that the British people would rise to the occasion – *'a people who will not flinch or weary of the struggle – hard and protracted though it will be'*. The eels were getting used to being skinned. *'Our qualities and deeds must burn and glow through the gloom of*

*Europe until they become the veritable beacon of its
salvation.'* And as he told the French in a BBC
broadcast in October, *'We are waiting for the long
promised invasion. So are the fishes.'* (By then Hitler
had postponed the invasion, to the next year at least.)

Group Captain, RAF, Frederick Winterbotham
recollected an evening in the Whitehall bunker with
Churchill during an air raid.

> . . . the whole of Carlton House Terrace, just across the
> park from where we were, was in flames, and the bombs
> were dropping around. And Churchill came up smoking
> his cigar . . . in front of the door of the underground
> offices was a sort of concrete screen, and everybody
> tried to prevent him going out in front of that because
> there was so much metal flying about. Not a bit. He
> went out and I can see him today with his hands on his
> stick, and smoking his cigar. We were all in a very dim
> light, and standing behind him – the Chiefs of Staff and
> Ismay and myself and my chief – and Churchill saying,
> *'My God, we'll get the buggers for this.'*

Clementine Churchill tried in vain to persuade her
husband to remain in comparative safety – but was
firmly informed: *'When I was a child my nursemaid
could never prevent me from taking a walk in the park if
I wanted to do so. And now I'm a man Adolf Hitler
certainly won't.'*

During one air raid, instead of remaining down in the
underground Cabinet War Rooms recently constructed
for him at Storey's Gate in Whitehall, he went up to
watch from the roof. An air-raid warden came up to him
and shyly asked him to move. *'Why?'* said Churchill
belligerently, preparing to dig in his heels. 'Because, sir,

you're sitting on the smoke vent and the building's full of smoke.'

One winter's day, to divert him from the grimmer news of the Blitz, an aide showed him a newspaper article about an elderly gentleman who had been arrested in Hyde Park for making improper advances to a young girl in sub-zero temperatures. *'Over seventy-five, and below zero!'* the Prime Minister exclaimed. *'Makes you proud to be British.'*

In the early days of the Blitz, Churchill was driven to Canterbury where he went to view the cathedral being bolstered with sandbags. The Archbishop was gloomy, and so the Prime Minister attempted to bolster him up too: *'No matter how many close hits the Nazis may make, I feel sure the cathedral will survive.'* 'Ah, *close* hits . . . ,' said the Archbishop glumly. 'But what if we get a *direct* hit?'

'In that event,' the Prime Minister responded, losing patience, *'you will have to regard it, my dear Archbishop, as a divine summons.'*

In an attempt to cheer everybody up, in a speech to the House of Commons referring to the bombing during one specific night, 23 September, he remarked *'On that particular Thursday night 180 persons were killed in London as a result of 251 tons of bombs. That is to say, it took one ton of bombs to kill three-quarters of a person.'* Today that would be called spin-doctoring.

The bombing continued; not only London, but other cities and towns were at risk – Coventry was bombed on 14 November, with over 550 killed and its ancient cathedral gutted; two days later the RAF bombed Hamburg; and on the night of the 19th the Germans bombed Birmingham, killing over 1,300 people. And

Churchill continued to work at keeping up British morale. The American Ambassador, John G. Winant, wrote to Roosevelt in April 1941:

> The Prime Minister's method of conducting a campaign on what one might call a morale front is unique. He arrives at a town unannounced, is taken to the most seriously bombed area, leaves his automobile and starts walking through the streets without guards. The news of his presence spreads rapidly by word of mouth and before he has gone far crowds flock about him, and people call out to him, 'Hello, Winnie', 'Good old Winnie', 'You will never let us down', 'That's a man'.

'I would listen to him speak,' said the BBC engineer in charge of outside broadcasts, Robert Wood. 'When he'd finished, I would find that we hadn't had it after all, we still had a fighting chance, and, come what may, we were going to win.'

Chapter 11

The End
of the Beginning

I N THE COURSE OF 1941 the bombing raids died
down, the Blitz petering out in May. A late casualty
was the chamber of the House of Commons, which had
to be rebuilt – it could not be used again till 1950, until
which time the Commons moved into the House of
Lords, driving the peers into the tiny King's Robing
Room.

It was not a good year. In January British troops occupied the Libyan port of Tobruk, but a few months later it
was besieged by Italian forces with some German troops
for support. In April, Germany and Italy invaded
Yugoslavia; and German troops were sent to the assis-
tance of Italian forces in Greece. Greece surrendered to
Germany and a third evacuation of British troops (after
Norway and Dunkirk) had to be ordered. About a month
later came the evacuation from Crete. In the meantime
General Erwin Rommel, commanding the German
Afrika Korps sent to bolster the Italians in North Africa,
had arrived in Egypt on 25 April. A distraction was pro-
vided by Rudolf Hess, Hitler's third deputy, who, having
made a solo flight from Germany, landed by parachute,

in Scotland in May – claiming on his arrest that he had come to persuade the British government to make a peace agreement with Germany. *'This is one of those cases in which the imagination is baffled by the facts,'* Churchill commented to the Commons.

That the German army was marching inexorably towards Moscow as June drew to a close, must, however, have given Churchill some cause for hope. His chance had come to gain a new and powerful ally against Hitler.

With the Ribbentrop–Molotov non-aggression pact secretly signed in August 1939, between Nazi Germany and the Soviet Union, Churchill's hopes of an alliance with the Soviet Union looked decidedly uncertain, and they seemed to have been ended once and for all when the Red Army entered eastern Poland less than three weeks later. Yet, he remarked, *'This is not the first time that Russia has defected'* – clearly believing that it would not be the last, either. He made the famous broadcast: *'I cannot forecast to you the action of Russia. It is a riddle wrapped in a mystery inside an enigma; but perhaps there is a key. That key is Russian national interest.'* Moreover, in spite of its pact with Germany, Russia did not itself drop the idea of an alliance with Britain and France.

Not long after he became Prime Minister, Churchill appointed Stafford Cripps Ambassador to the Soviet Union. A Marxist, severely honest and sincere, and teetotal, he made Churchill feel uncomfortable – *'He has all the virtues I dislike and none of the vices I admire.'* In the USSR Cripps would be, the Prime Minister felt, *'a lunatic in a country of lunatics'*.

When Paris fell to the Germans in 1940, Molotov, the Russian Foreign Minister (who Churchill said resembled *'the modern concept of a robot'*), sent a telegram of congratulations to his German counterpart von Ribbentrop, and the Soviet press reported every British defeat at Nazi hands with satisfaction. At the same time the Russians were deeply suspicious of Nazi Germany and hoped that their occupation of bordering countries would build up some sort of defence against Hitler. The Soviet Union was also engaged at that time in border disputes with Japan – it now seemed a wise move to end hostilities with Japan, and on 13 April 1941, the two countries signed a five-year neutrality pact.

On 22 June 1941, Germany invaded the Soviet Union, taking Stalin, and all Russia, by surprise. *'At four o'clock this morning Hitler attacked and invaded Russia,'* Churchill announced in a BBC broadcast. *'All his usual formalities of perfidy were observed with scrupulous technique . . .'* On that same day Italy and Romania declared war on the USSR. At once, international affairs were transformed.

Churchill greeted the news with satisfaction. *'If Hitler invaded hell I would make at least a favourable reference to the Devil in the House of Commons,'* he had declared only the day before (he had once remarked to Leo Amery that God must exist because of *'the existence of Lenin and Trotsky for whom a hell is needed'*). The USSR would make a useful ally. On 12 July Britain and the Soviet Union signed a treaty of mutual aid – although there was in fact little that Britain could do to help Russia other than send supplies.

A few days later Churchill travelled by destroyer in the company of Roosevelt's aide, Harry Hopkins, to Newfoundland for a meeting with the President. At dinner the first evening, he opened a pot of caviar, a present from Stalin. *'Ah, Mr Hopkins,'* he said, *'it is good to have such a treat, even if it means fighting on the side of the Russians to get it.'*

Although he got on with Stalin – indeed, he seemed to have a blind spot about him, speaking admiringly of his wisdom, courage and humour – he had no illusions about 'that monster' the Soviet leader's motives. At the Yalta Conference in February 1945, following Roosevelt's tribute to the Soviet leader, Churchill was persuaded by an aide to follow suit (objecting the while: *'But they do not want peace'*). Getting to his feet, he proposed a toast to *'Premier Stalin, whose conduct of foreign policy manifests a desire for peace.'* Then, in a whispered aside out of the interpreter's hearing: *'A piece of Poland, a piece of Czechoslovakia, a piece of Romania . . .'*

But that was later – against Nazi Germany it was useful to have the huge Soviet Union as an ally. To have the United States – still neutral – would be a whole lot better. *'The Russian danger* [from the Nazis] *is our danger and the danger of the United States . . .'* Churchill said pointedly in a broadcast.

Although even before the war President Roosevelt had expressed at least moral support for Britain in her stand against Hitler, that was as far as it went to begin with. His Ambassador to Great Britain, Joseph P. Kennedy (father of John F.) – perhaps not that good a choice for the post as his Irish-American biases meant that he was not entirely sympathetic towards Britain – advised Roosevelt against joining the war on the grounds that Germany was bound to defeat Britain.

Churchill, however, had built up a close relationship with Roosevelt (whom he had met in 1918), and was in constant touch with him. In July 1940 he asked Roosevelt for *'fifty or sixty of your oldest destroyers'*, which the President agreed to send. In August Churchill announced plans to lease bases in British colonies to the United States – *'Undoubtedly this process means that these two great organizations . . . the British Empire and the United States, will have to be somewhat mixed up together in some of their affairs . . .'* He was a wily old bird. A couple of months later Roosevelt released 250,000 rifles to the British army. And next came his Lend-Lease Bill, under which the US would supply Britain with vital materials – including aircraft – to be paid for at a later date. *'Give us the tools, and we'll finish the job,'* said Churchill in February 1941; the US Congress passed the Lend-Lease Act on 11 March. On 4 August the two heads of state had that secret meeting in Newfoundland (Roosevelt pretending he was going on a fishing trip). 'The United States will wage war but not declare it' was Roosevelt's message; on the 14th they signed the Atlantic Charter. The two nations were committed to 'the final destruction of the Nazi tyranny', with the rider that 'all the nations of the world, for realistic as well as spiritual reasons, must come to the abandonment of the use of force'.

Then, on 7 December, came Japan's attack on Pearl Harbor. (Which pleased Churchill as he knew that the States would now join the Allies.) That evening he was at Chequers with Averell Harriman, Roosevelt's personal representative, and John Winant, who had replaced Kennedy as US Ambassador, when they heard on the wireless 'something about the Japanese attacking the Americans'. According to Winant, Churchill jumped to his feet, announcing *'We shall declare war on Japan.'*

Winant replied: 'Good God, you can't declare war on a radio announcement.' Churchill immediately telephoned the President and assured him that Britain's declaration of war would follow close behind that of the United States.

The Japanese rapidly followed up this action by invading most of the countries of South-East Asia, including British colonies such as Singapore and Malaya. As Churchill was to remark in a speech to the House of Commons in January 1942: *'The Japanese, whose game is what I may call to make hell while the sun shines.'* Congress declared war on Japan on the 8th, and on the 11th Germany and Italy declared war on the United States.

Australia, which in 1939 had sent armed forces to Britain's aid, were now cut off from Britain and, worried by the possibility of a Japanese invasion, sought alliance with the United States – which in turn used Australia as a base for military operations.

Not long after, Churchill went to Canada to assure himself of the Canadians' continued participation – or to assure them of ultimate victory. He told them that when, in 1940, he had said to the French that whatever they did, Britain would continue to fight on alone, *'their generals'* had commented that in three weeks Britain would have *'her neck wrung like a chicken'*. He waited while the Canadians absorbed this, then added, *'Some chicken! . . . Some neck!'* They roared their appreciation – and he could be sure of their support.

Over the next three years Churchill travelled – to Moscow, to Cairo, to Casablanca, Washington, DC, Algiers, Tehran, Quebec . . . No longer a young man, it is scarcely surprising, especially given the circumstances, that his health gave way from time to time. Considerations of health, though, were of less importance to the Prime Minister than was his being actively involved on all possible fronts. If he went somewhere for a conference he made sure that if British troops happened to be stationed nearby he also went to see them. While he was in Washington, it is related by Roosevelt's speechwriter, the dramatist Robert E. Sherwood, in his 1948 Pulitzer Prize-winning biography *Roosevelt and Hopkins* (or *The White Papers of Harry L. Hopkins*), Roosevelt was so eager to continue discussions that he hurried his wheelchair into Churchill's room, to find his guest, as Hopkins put it, 'stark naked and gleaming pink from his bath'. Roosevelt hastened to put his wheelchair into reverse, but heard the words: *'Pray'* – a favourite expression of Churchill's – *'enter – the Prime Minister of Great Britain has nothing to hide from the President of the United States.'* When, on 30 January 1942, he sent a birthday greeting to the American President, the answer came back: 'It is fun to be in the same decade with you.'

The first months of 1942 continued with bleak news for the new Allies. In North Africa Rommel, the 'Desert Fox', still had the upper hand against Allied troops; in January the Japanese captured Kuala Lumpur, the capital of Malaya; and in February, forced the British garrison at Singapore to surrender; three German battle cruisers escaped from Brest and breezed home up the English Channel on 12 February – which angered many even more than the loss of Singapore. And Churchill faced a no-confidence vote in the Commons, which did little for his morale at such a time. However, he won the vote, and Rommel's advance was stopped by General

Auchinleck in June – which meant that Cairo was saved, and thus all Egypt, and with it Britain's vital link to the Persian oilfields.

Many of Churchill's trips were to discuss various plans to invade Nazi-held territory across the English Channel, and also in Norway and French North Africa. He held several meetings with Roosevelt, and he also visited Stalin in Moscow; and of course he spent many hours with General de Gaulle, leader of the Free French.

In August 1942 came the Dieppe fiasco. An Allied raid, perhaps ill-prepared – and certainly owing some of its failure to its planners' under-estimate of enemy strength – resulted in disaster in German-occupied Dieppe with many Allied servicemen, predominantly Canadians, killed, wounded or captured. This, as Churchill later pointed out, served only to intensify the Germans' consciousness of the threat from across the Channel.

Churchill involved himself in military matters as well, and in what might today be called 'hiring and firing' military leaders. He appointed General William Gott as commander of the Eighth Army, having decided that Auchinleck, who had taken personal command of the Eighth Army and halted Rommel at the first battle of El Alamein, was being slow and indecisive; Gott was killed in an accident the next day and the post went to Montgomery, while Auchinleck was offered command in Iraq and Persia in place of General Wavell. General Alexander, C-in-C Near East Command, then replaced Auchinleck as C-in-C Middle East. In November Generals Alexander and Montgomery were able to report victory in the second battle of El Alamein –

Churchill was delighted, though cautiously so: *'This is not the end. It is not even the beginning of the end. But it is, perhaps, the end of the beginning.'* All over Britain, church bells were ringing.

'They say I interfered during the war,' Churchill later said to Robert Boothby. *'I did. I interfered all the time.'*

'Without him my efforts would have been futile from the start,' de Gaulle wrote of Churchill (whom he had been known to refer to as 'le monstre de Downing Street') in his memoirs. 'By lending me a strong and willing hand when he did, [he] vitally aided the cause of France.'

Churchill and Roosevelt quite often found the Frenchman's behaviour somewhat difficult, however. At the Casablanca Conference in January 1943, Roosevelt, according to a US Foreign Policy Document, at one point turned despairingly to Churchill: 'I do not know what to do with de Gaulle.' To which the Prime Minister replied, *'I am no more enamoured with him than you are, but I would rather have him on the committee than strutting about as a combination of Joan of Arc and Clemenceau.'*

At this conference, General de Gaulle tried to claim for the Free French gold, rescued from France, and held in a blocked account at the Bank of England. Churchill had been told not to discuss it with the General but to leave it to the experts – and for once he did as he was told, explaining kindly to a thoroughly baffled and possibly slightly scandalized de Gaulle that *'Quand je me trouve en face de la Vieille Dame de Threadneedle Street, je me trouve toujours impotent.'* (The word he needed was 'impuissant' – powerless, rather than 'impotent'.) Churchill was later to comment (after the General had come to visit him over the New Year break): '*Now that the General speaks English so well he understands my French perfectly.*'

Securing the wholehearted compliance of the French during the war was not always easy, especially when it required the co-operation of both de Gaulle and the collaborationist Vichy French. Urged by a diplomat to massage de Gaulle's pride with flattery, Churchill is said to have to have agreed: '*I'll kiss him on both cheeks – or, if you prefer, on all four.*'

While at Casablanca, Churchill thought he might do a little sight-seeing and expressed an interest in strolling through the Kasbah. This caused alarm among his security guards, who could not guarantee his safety in such a place. Knowing, however, that Churchill would not be swayed by considerations of his personal safety, they earnestly pointed out to him that the Kasbah was an unhealthy place where he might contract some terrible oriental infection – which he might even pass on to the President of the United States. Wickedly, the Prime Minister chose to play along with them, and also to carry matters a bit further . . . '*Ah ha! So you think there's life in the old dog yet, do you? I assure you, my friends, that even if I were to go to the Kasbah and contract the disease which you have in mind, I should be most unlikely to communicate it to the President.*'

Next, as 1943 drew to a close, came the Tehran Conference with Stalin, whom Churchill and Roosevelt had to tell that they had decided to postpone 'Second Front', the invasion of Europe that they had been planning. Stalin was deeply suspicious. They did their best to make clear to him that they wanted, first, compete success in their Italian campaign, which had been launched on 10 July after the successful Anglo-American invasions of, first, Sicily and, then, mainland Italy, where the Germans continued fighting. On the 25th the King of Italy had asked for Mussolini's resignation and placed him in military custody. Marshal Pietro Badoglio formed a new ministry and soon decreed the liquidation of all Fascist organizations.

At another conference – in Quebec, in August – Churchill managed to obtain Roosevelt's agreement to set up South-East Asia Command with Admiral Lord Louis ('Dickie') Mountbatten as its Supreme Commander. Mountbatten recollected the occasion at a talk to the Churchill Centre. Then Chief of Combined Operations, responsible for amphibious operations against German forces in Occupied Europe, he had accompanied Churchill to Canada for the Quebec Conference, and was summoned by him to the Citadel:

> '*What do you think about the situation in South-East Asia?*' he asked. 'It stinks, doesn't it?' I said. '*What do you mean?*' he enquired. 'Everything is wrong,' I replied. 'They've lost their morale, got no priorities – they've been defeated on land, at sea and in the air continuously. It's pretty hopeless.' '*Do you think you can put it right?*' asked Winston. Of course I thought that he meant I should go out on a fact-finding mission and write a report. 'I'm much too busy,' I replied. '*You don't understand,*' Winston snapped. '*The President and I want you to go out and set up a Supreme Allied Command and then run it.*' . . . Winston gave me the most terrific support all the way through – at a time when we had no priorities, the main hope we got was from Winston.

Mountbatten (whom Churchill described as *'a triphibian – equally at home on land, sea or air; and he has experienced a bit of fire too'*), backed by Auchinleck, now C-in-C India, was able to support General Sir William Slim, commanding the Fourteenth Army, in his campaign to stop the Japanese from invading north-eastern India, and in eventually driving them back into Burma and completely defeating them there. In September 1945 Mountbatten received the Japanese surrender in Singapore.

At the Quebec Conference, Churchill also secured Roosevelt's agreement to the formation of the rather unorthodox corps of British, Burmese, and Gurkha commandos under the leadership (until his death in 1944) of the eccentric Orde Wingate (whom Churchill saw as another T. E. Lawrence) – a package that appealed to Churchill's romantic imagination. Known as the Chindits, after the dragon-like statues (*chinthe*) guarding Burmese temples, their daring guerrilla strikes dealt a significant blow to the Japanese operations in Burma and advance on British-held India. Destroying bridges, military installations, ammunition dumps, and railway lines on their way, by 1944 they had infiltrated deep into Japanese-held territory, where they relayed intelligence to the RAF. With their backing, Slim was able to take the Burmese capital of Rangoon less than a week before VE-Day. The plan was to go on to Malaya and Singapore, but in the event that proved to be unnecessary.

On 3 September 1943 Badoglio, the *de facto* Italian leader, signed an armistice, which set off a furious race between the Allies and the Germans for possession of all the other military facilities that had been under Italian control, including bases, communications, arms and supplies. German commandos had plucked Mussolini from captivity in September and announced a Fascist National Government, established in the German-held North of Italy, under his leadership in opposition to the Badoglio government. In the meantime Badoglio declared war on Germany on 13 October. It would be a while before the Allies were able to sort Italy out – but at least they now had another ally.

'Operation Overlord', the long-awaited Allied invasion of Europe, came about at last on 6 June 1944 – D-Day. De Gaulle decided to be difficult, bristling because he had not been told earlier about the plans to invade – to liberate – his own country. Churchill wrote: *'I had expected that de Gaulle would dine with us and come back to London . . . but he drew himself up and stated that he preferred to motor . . . separately.'*

Churchill, of course, wanted to be there when the troops landed in Normandy – General Eisenhower, the Supreme Commander, failed to dissuade him, and only a letter from the King stopped him. So he spent the day in the Commons, but was soon to visit commanders and troops in France.

The Allied advance from the Normandy beachhead was swift, and Paris was finally liberated on 25 August 1944, to the overwhelming joy of the French people. De Gaulle was recognized as head of the new French government.

That summer and autumn London came under attack from, first, German flying bombs, and then German V2 rockets. At about the same time US Army units were pushing their way into Germany. The war was not over.

And even where the Germans had been defeated there was trouble – as in Italy, and in Athens where Communist forces had thrown themselves into the fray; and of course the Far East, where the Japanese continued fighting. Churchill continued on his difficult journeys – to Italy, to Quebec again, to Moscow, to Paris, to Athens. Even his beloved Chief of Staff, General Ismay, suffered the backlash of his temper as the strain began to tell, although the Prime Minister's contrition was immediate. Ismay wrote in a letter home dated 15 September:

> Master has been extraordinarily difficult – so much so that . . . I wrote yesterday offering to resign. He dealt with it in typical fashion: handed it back to me saying, 'Don't write me this sort of rubbish, dear Pug: we are going to the end – together – you and I. I'm sorry if I get angry, but you must admit I have cause.' I replied that he had abundant cause, but why vent it all on me! And why give me the feeling that I could do nothing right. He denied this: said he had every confidence in me, and was much dependent on my industry, tact and judgement . . .

Athens was a bit of a stumbling block for Churchill; he was determined to oust the Communist Resistance groups and was criticized by both the American and the British press (but not, thanks to Stalin, the Soviet press). Eventually he went there, at the end of the year, for discussions with the leading factions, which led to a compromise settlement in January 1945.

The German armies were retreating – but apart from the need to defeat Japan, Roosevelt and Churchill had the task of negotiating with Stalin about the USSR's post-war borders. The Americans were particularly anxious that the Soviet Union should fight against Japan – and were not too concerned about what Stalin did in Eastern Europe. In the end Churchill had to agree that Russia should have control of Romania and Bulgaria, and influence in the Polish government, but not Greece. Robert Boothby later wrote: 'At Yalta whole nations had been handed around like plums, without any regard to their own wishes. "All right, old boy," they said, over the caviar, vodka and cigars. "We'll give you Bulgaria and Romania if you give us Greece."'

As Churchill pointed out later, however, in defence of Yalta, Germany was not yet beaten and they could not quarrel with the might of Russia. Japan was not beaten either.

It was the last time that Churchill was to see Roosevelt, who died in April, to the Prime Minister's – and the free world's – deep sorrow.

In February 1945 the RAF's Bomber Command under Air Chief Marshal Sir Arthur Harris, and the US Army Air Force, bombed Dresden over three days, killing some 135,000 people and destroying 80 per cent of the city. The following month, on 28 March, Churchill sent a minute to his Chiefs of Staff advising that it was time to review the bombing policy *'otherwise we shall come into control of an utterly ruined land . . . The destruction of Dresden remains a serious query against the conduct of Allied bombing . . . I feel the need for more precise concentration upon military objectives, such as oil and communications behind the immediate battle-zone, rather than on mere acts of terror and wanton destruction, however impressive.'* This minute – with its sentiments so relevant today – was not long after replaced by a more blandly worded and impersonal one.

According to his biographer, Martin Gilbert, when he was watching an Air Ministry film of the still smouldering ruins of German cities devastated by British bombers, he suddenly said, *'Are we beasts? Are we taking this too far?'* In his history of the war, Churchill, perhaps shamefacedly, referred to the attack on Dresden as *'a heavy raid'* on a *'centre of communications'.*

According to his 'shadow', Inspector Thompson, when Churchill visited Generals Eisenhower and Montgomery on the west bank of the Rhine in March, he picked up a shell and, taking a piece of chalk lying nearby, wrote on it: *'FOR HITLER PERSONALLY!'*

It wasn't needed. On 30 April, as the Red Army marched into Berlin, Hitler killed his mistress, his dog, and himself. Churchill, when he heard from Jock Colville that German radio had announced that Hitler had died 'fighting with his last breath against Bolshevism,' remarked, *'Well, I must say I think he was perfectly right to die like that.'*

On the morning of 7 May, the German High Command signed an unconditional surrender.

'That's it!' exclaimed Ismay in triumph. *'Yes,'* said the Prime Minister. *'The eagle has ceased to scream, but the parrots will now begin to chatter. The war of the giants is over and the pygmies will now begin to squabble.'*

Chapter 12

An Iron Curtain

As EARLY AS 1944, Harold Laski, the left-wing political scientist – who had recently been elected vice-chairman of the National Executive Committee of the Labour party – suggested that a fund should be raised in token of the nation's gratitude to its Prime Minister. Churchill thanked Laski and, noting the rather valedictory tone, remarked that things of that kind were better left until a man is dead. *'If, however, when I am dead, people think of commemorating my services,'* he went on, *'I should like to think that a park was made for the children of London's poor on the south bank of the Thames, where they have suffered so grimly from the Hun.'* Most of the area he probably had in mind has been rebuilt, without a park.

With victory won in Europe and victory over Japan looking equally certain as the Japanese forces were being pushed back, many in the government – especially the Labour Party – felt that it was time to put an end to the wartime coalition government and hold a general election. Churchill spent most of his time preparing for the three-party conference on the future of Europe to be held in the German city of Potsdam, near Berlin; much of his election campaign took the form of triumphant victory speeches. Polling day was on 5 July 1945, but results were not due for some three weeks as the votes of the troops scattered abroad had to be collected. Churchill was very tired, unsurprisingly, and now that the dangers were over after such a long and difficult fight, he fell into a state of post-climactic lassitude. So he flew to France with members of his family for a brief holiday, before going on to Berlin for the Potsdam Conference on 15 July.

There he met the new US President, Harry S. Truman, for the first time. He had, however, been in touch with him previously – and on 12 May had sent him a message which included his perception of the stance being taken by Soviets: *'An iron curtain is drawn down upon their front. We do not know what is going on behind . . .'*

This was not the first time he used that phrase (he'd used it in *The World Crisis*), and not the last – he used it again on 4 June to Truman, and at Potsdam, he complained to Stalin that an 'iron fence' had come down on the British mission in Bucharest. Most famously, he used it in his 'Sinews of Peace' speech at Fulton, Missouri, in 1946. It is not a phrase original to him, but one he picked up on and made the most of. Goebbels had used it only a few months before in a warning to the German people of what would descend upon them if they surrendered to the Soviets (he was not wrong); it had been used a number of times before, by, among others, German-born Queen Elisabeth of Belgium in 1914 ('Between [the Germans] and me there is now a bloody iron curtain which has descended forever!');

Ethel Snowden (wife of Churchill's erstwhile colleague Philip Snowden) in a 1920 book about travelling through Russia just after the Revolution; and, apparently, by the Earl of Munster in his journal in 1817. It took Churchill to make the phrase famous.

In 1924, in his article 'Shall We All Commit Suicide?' (in *Nash's Pall Mall*), Churchill wrote, with startling prescience, *'Might not a bomb no bigger than an orange be found to possess secret power to destroy a whole block of buildings, nay, to blast a township at a stroke? Could not explosives . . . be guided automatically in flying machines . . .?'*

It was not until the 1930s that scientists began to see how a hitherto inconceivably powerful bomb could be developed by the fission of uranium. In 1939 Albert Einstein wrote to President Roosevelt about the work he and his colleagues were carrying out – and also saying that he believed that similar work was being carried out in Germany. Roosevelt had discussed the bomb's development with Churchill on several occasions during the previous couple of years. But it was on 16 July 1945, during the Potsdam Conference, that the first test of an atomic bomb was carried out and it was proved to work. Churchill and Truman agreed that they might use it against Japan (ostensibly partly on the grounds that the Japanese might have themselves developed the bomb and would not hesitate to use it). On the 26th Truman mentioned to Stalin a 'new weapon of unusual destructive force'; Stalin apparently slipped off to telephone his scientists and tell them to hurry up.

The first atomic bomb (a uranium bomb) was dropped on Hiroshima on 6 August. The implications started becoming clear quickly. 'An impenetrable cloud of dust and smoke, standing over the ruin of the great Japanese arsenal at Hiroshima, still veils the undoubtedly stupendous destruction wrought by the first impact in war of the atomic bomb,' wrote the author of a *Times* leader article published on the 8th. 'Imagination shudders at the thought that this terrifying power might have fallen into the hands of the enemies of civilization instead of its protectors,' continued the article. 'Reason will tell mankind that war is becoming with certainty suicidal' ('Shall we all commit suicide?'), and it ended expressing the hope 'that the new power be consecrated to peace and not to war . . . [it] is a choice set before the conscience of humanity; and in a terrible and most literal sense it is a choice of life or death.' So a plutonium bomb was dropped on Nagasaki on the 9th. Japan surrendered on the 14th.

Two days later Churchill defended the bombing in a speech to the Commons, arguing that had the Germans or Japanese discovered the new weapon they would have used it on the Allies *'with the utmost alacrity'*. And would have annihilated them. There were many who had reservations, and as the effect of the bombings continued to become apparent over the decades, many more. Asked how he would face his Maker over the dropping of the bombs, Churchill was heard to reply, *'I shall defend myself with resolution and with vigour. I shall say to the Almighty, why when nations were warring in this way, did You release this dangerous knowledge to mankind? The fault is Yours – not mine!'*

In his last major speech to the Commons in March 1955, with reference to deterrence, he expressed the hope that *'Safety will be the sturdy child of terror, and survival the twin brother of annihilation.'*

Two or three years later, in the late 1950s, Churchill and Anthony Montague Browne were invited by the Director of the Atomic Weapons Research Establishment to see their work at Aldermaston; they were also shown films of the tests carried out on the Christmas Islands and Montebello. On the way home Churchill was silent; after a while he asked Montague Browne what he'd thought; his companion murmured something vague and asked him what *he* had thought. *'If I were God Almighty, and humanity blew itself to bits, as it most certainly could, I don't think that I'd start again in case they got me too next time,'* Churchill replied. *'I always feared,'* he went on, *'that mass pressure in the United States might force them to use their H-bombs while the Russians still had not got any.'* Then, unable to resist making a joke: *'It's always been a tendency of the masses to drop their Hs.'*

The election results were due on the 26th and Churchill left Potsdam on the 25th to be in London to hear the result. The general view was that he would win because he had won the war for Britain. That morning, just before dawn, Churchill claimed in *The Second World War*, he was woken *'with a sharp stab of almost physical pain'* and the conviction that he was beaten.

By midday it was confirmed – the electorate felt that for peacetime the Labour Party had more to offer; Churchill was now Leader of the Opposition, and Clement Attlee (whom Churchill famously described as *'a sheep in sheep's clothing'*) was Prime Minister. According to his daughter, Mary Soames, in her biography of her mother, Clementine – who probably thought it was high time her husband had some rest and spent 'more time with his family' – his wife said to him at lunch: 'It may well be a blessing in disguise.' To which he replied, *'At the moment it seems quite effectively disguised.'* Churchill was very disappointed – there was unfinished business to deal with – he had not yet finished saving the world. But he said, nevertheless, *'I thank the British people for many kindnesses shown towards their servant.'*

Stalin's reaction when Churchill returned to Potsdam with the new Prime Minister was allegedly one of surprise that he had not 'fixed' the election.

According to Kay Halle, in *The Irrepressible Churchill*, at about that time some boors who had managed to get hold of a hand grenade threw it into his fish pond at Chartwell killing all his beloved carp. Lindemann was heard to say, 'I think it's the dirtiest, filthiest, most cowardly thing I ever heard – what happened to those fish.'

'Oh,' said Churchill, *'I thought you were going to allude to the elections.'*

Not long after his defeat, George VI offered him the Order of the Garter. *'I could not accept the Order of the Garter from my sovereign,'* remarked Churchill, *'when I have received the order of the boot from his people.'* (It was eventually conferred upon him by Queen Elizabeth in 1953, just before her coronation; he was to refuse a dukedom.)

Now leader of the Opposition, Churchill fell back on a lifestyle not dissimilar to that of his so-called wilderness years, the decade up to 1939. He travelled widely, he talked a great deal and was a nuisance in the Commons; he uttered dire prophecies – but this time about the

Soviet Union; he worked on writing his history of the war; and, for relaxation, he painted.

In the House of Commons he was outspoken in his criticism of the government and its ministers. *'No government has ever combined so passionate a lust for power with such curious impotence in its exercise,'* he declared to the House of Commons.

Churchill's spats with Herbert Morrison, the Leader of the House and, according to Churchill, *'a curious mixture of geniality and venom',* occurred so regularly that they became known as 'Children's Hour'. Churchill: *'Mr Herbert Morrison is a master craftsman.'* Morrison: 'The Right Hon. gentleman has promoted me.' Churchill: *'Craft is common to both skill and deceit.'*

Stafford Cripps and Aneurin (Nye) Bevan also came under attack. The ascetic, teetotal Cripps must have been an uncomfortable figure to have around for someone like Churchill, who was shameless in his indulgence in luxury and drink; indeed, as Jock Colville put it, Cripps 'was also suspected of believing that the hair shirts which he chose for his own wardrobe should be manufactured and distributed to the whole community'. Apparently, however, he allowed himself one luxury – smoking cigars – until he forswore that, too, announcing the move as an example of the kind of sacrifice expected of the nation in a time of post-war austerity.

Churchill was heard to remark, *'Too bad – that was his last contact with humanity.'*

Nye Bevan, MP for Ebbw Vale (*'He will be as great a curse to this country in peace as he was a squalid nuisance in time of war'*), as Minister of Health, was instrumental in establishing the National Health Service. Churchill was heard once to refer to Bevan as *'a merchant of discourtesy'*, and was himself not inclined to be courteous towards Bevan. *'I can think of no better step to signal the inauguration of the National Health Service than that a person who so obviously needs psychiatric attention should be among the first of its patients,'* he declared. And in July 1952 – back in the driving seat – Churchill, in a speech concerning British recognition of communist China, pointed out: *'If you recognize anyone, it does not mean that you like him. We all, for instance, recognize the Honourable Member for Ebbw Vale.'*

He was also sometimes pretty rude about the Prime Minister, Clem Attlee, whom he saw as an insubstantial figure – *'a modest man who has a good deal to be modest about'*. When he heard that the Prime Minister had cancelled a planned trip to Australia, he couldn't resist remarking, *'He is afraid that when the mouse is away the cats will play.'*

It is not surprising that he was held to be the originator of the wisecrack that was circulating the early post-war corridors of Whitehall: *'An empty taxi arrived at 10 Downing Street, and when the door was opened Attlee got out.'* When, however, Jock Colville repeated it and its attribution to him, Churchill's face stiffened and 'after an awful pause', he said: *'Mr Attlee is an honourable and gallant gentleman, and a faithful colleague who served his country well at the time of her greatest need. I should be obliged if you would make it clear whenever an occasion arises that I would never make such a remark about him, and that I strongly disapprove of anybody who does.'* The vehemence and pomposity of this denial suggest that perhaps Churchill *was* responsible for the jest, but, whether as a matter of conscience or for some other personal reason, was immediately anxious to disown it. Perhaps he felt that it was going too far – on leaving office not long before, he had assured his Private Secretary, Paul Beards, that 'Mr Attlee is a very nice man.'

Somehow, a remark he made in a letter to a cousin about volume IV of his history, *The Second World War*, being '*a worse tyrant than Attlee*' leaves one unconvinced of its tyranny. But his writing made a tyrant of *him*. As Martin Gilbert relates, while working on his book in Aix-en-Provence, he suddenly decided he needed Bill Deakin, his research assistant, the respected historian, and telephoned him: '*Bill, I am very hard-pressed. I want you to come down right away. Take tomorrow's plane. I'll have a car meet you at the airport.*'

'I'm so sorry, sir, but I can't get away that early. I have a lot of work to wind up at Oxford and can't leave for at least four days.'

'*What's that you say? I can't hear you. I need you down here. Get on the plane as fast you can. We'll arrange everything from this end.*'

'But, sir, I said I can't possibly do it. There is work I must finish up here first.'

'*This connection is very bad. Can't hear a word you say. We'll see you tomorrow, then. Goodbye.*'

A minor stroke suffered in the autumn of 1949 – possibly the first of many – did not stop him from working on his huge book. He was in the habit of submitting draft chapters for comment to a wide variety of people, including his wife, who on one occasion announced at dinner, 'I have now finished volume three and I hope you will pay some attention to the little notes

I have made in the margins. You must make a great many changes. I got so tired of the endless detail about unimportant battles and incidents. So much of the material is pedestrian.'

In 1947 he was overheard in an authors' exchange with Lord Beaverbrook: *'What are you up to at the moment?'*

'Writing a book,' answered Beaverbrook.

'Hmm. What are you writing about?'

'Me.'

'A good subject,' Churchill said approvingly. *'I've been writing about me for fifty years, and with excellent results.'*

The first volume of *The Second World War* was published in 1948, the last one, volume VI, in 1954. The epigraph to the work reads:

> *In war: resolution*
> *In defeat: defiance*
> *In victory: magnanimity*
> *In peace: goodwill.*

Churchill, seemingly still not content to stay in one place for any length of time travelled extensively over the next five or so years – often to pick up a degree or honour. He was made a freeman of some fifty towns and cities from Thebes to Cap d'Ail to Harrow; he was Lord Warden of the Cinque Ports and Grand Master of the Primrose League; at Aachen in 1956 he was awarded the Charlemagne Prize for services to Europe, at Aachen (he was astonished to be cheered as he was driven through the streets of Aachen and Bonn); he was made Grand Seigneur of the Company of Adventurers of England into Hudson's Bay; he was the first non-

American to receive the Freedom Award; in 1958 he was decorated by General de Gaulle with the Cross of Liberation; and he was presented with honorary citizenship of the United States of America, declared by proclamation at a ceremony at the White House on 9 April 1963. And of course there was his Order of the Garter (and the dukedom he turned down). Over the years he received honorary degrees from some twenty universities. In February 1946 (a month before his famous 'Iron Curtain' speech), he was given a degree at Miami University and remarked, *'One might say that no one ever passed so few exams and received so many degrees.'* It was less than five years since his famous tribute to the RAF pilots of the Battle of Britain.

While devoting much energy to the concept of a united Europe, in part to stand up to the Soviet bogeyman, Churchill also liked to stress the 'special relationship' (his phrase, now beloved of recent British governments) between the United States and Britain, formalized in the Atlantic Charter and meant to include all the English-speaking nations. His greatest concern was the Soviet Union. When President Truman invited him to speak at Fulton's Westminster College (*'Westminster . . . that has a familiar ring to it'*) in March 1946, Americans were divided as to what the US policy towards the Soviet Union should be. There were those who saw Stalin as a protector of Russian security, and those who believed that he was bent on expansion by force. Churchill's speech – which became known as the 'Iron Curtain' speech – created a furore with the strength of its warning against the Soviet Union. *'From Stettin in the Baltic to Trieste in the Adriatic, an iron curtain has descended across the continent . . .'*

In Harold Macmillan's words, he 'shook and even shocked American opinion . . . Was it restlessness? Was it disappointment over his loss of office? Or – unpleasant thought – could he perhaps be right? After all, he had been right before.' The speech caused a stir throughout the world. *'I do not believe that Soviet Russia desires war,'* Churchill told his audience. *'What they desire is the fruits of war and the indefinite expansion of their power and doctrines.'* And he called for *'a good understanding on all points with Russia'.*

Little advance was made. There was the Truman Doctrine the following year, which initially had the aim of giving poor countries material aid so that poverty would not lead them to submit to bolshevism. And there was the Assembly of Strasbourg which Churchill helped to found. Macmillan described him at the first meeting in 1949 sitting 'between two Italians with whom he conversed volubly and audibly in his characteristic French'. It was just after that that Churchill suffered his first stroke, which was successfully concealed from the press and the public. It did little to slow him down.

He was, once again, accused of warmongering – and as an election approached in 1951, the Labour Minister Hugh Dalton predicted, 'If we get Churchill and the Tory Party back at the next election we shall be at war with Russia within twelve months.'

He was wrong. In one of his election speeches, Churchill said, *'If I remain in public life . . . it is because . . . I believe I may be able to make an important contribution to the prevention of a third world war . . . It is the last prize I seek to win.'* He won with a small majority. Churchill was back, but there was no war with Russia.

Chapter 13

Immortally Young

SHORTLY BEFORE THE ELECTION the fourth volume of *The Second World War* was published. The reviews were excellent. 'Mr Churchill's true genius is not epic but dramatic. The essence of tragedy lies in reversal of fortune. So also does that of comedy, and Mr Churchill, with the youthful zest which has carried him unfatigued through half a century of public life, here misses no opportunity of picking out the little comic things in the midst of the sorrows and terrors of war,' said *The Times*.

'It is a breathtaking book,' wrote the *Times Literary Supplement*'s reviewer. 'To say that Mr Churchill is a romantic, as immortally young as the hero of *Treasure Island*, is not to lose sight of the massive common sense of his judgement at the grimmest moments or his superhuman resilience in facing the ugliest facts squarely and taking tremendous decisions. It is rather to point at one deep source of his strength.'

Both reviewers picked up on the youthfulness, and Churchill himself, approaching his seventy-eighth birthday, impressed people with his youthful zest. The

Chairman of the Woodford Conservative Association found his electioneering zeal a bit exasperating: '. . . our schedules are invariably organized by the candidate himself, as his mounting and infectious enthusiasm leads him to make many more stops and many more speeches than we plan . . .'

As Prime Minister again, he set about putting together his Cabinet – as he once said, *'Reconstructing a Cabinet is like solving a kaleidoscopic jigsaw puzzle.'* He filled it mostly with people he knew well – himself as Minister of Defence, but only until the following year; his son-in-law, Duncan Sandys, became Minister of Supply; (another son-in-law, Christopher Soames, was made Parliamentary Private Secretary); Lindemann (now Lord Cherwell) became Paymaster-General; Field Marshal Alexander (made 1st Earl of Tunis in 1952) replaced Churchill as Minister of Defence in 1952, having been hauled back from Canada where he was Governor-General; Anthony Eden was given back his wartime post as Secretary of State for Foreign Affairs; his friend Pug – Lord Ismay since 1947 – became Secretary of State for Commonwealth Relations (and in 1952 he was appointed Secretary-General to the North Atlantic Treaty Organization – NATO); R. A. (Rab) Butler, who had been Minister of Education during Churchill's previous premiership, became Chancellor of the Exchequer.

Many of Churchill's meetings with his ministers took place in his bedroom, with him presiding from the comfort of his bed and Toby his budgerigar flying around and doing exactly what he wanted. Jock Colville recalled one occasion when Rab Butler had to spend a long time with Churchill going through Budget papers;

at the end of the session Colville counted fourteen budgie droppings on the Chancellor's balding head.

Many thought that Churchill should never have had a second term as Prime Minister. Yet it was not a disaster; neither was he. But he was definitely a wartime premier, and too long had passed since his days as a peacetime minister. He tended to leave matters he was unsure of to civil servants – 'the boys'. He told Harold Macmillan, his Minister of Housing, to '"*build the houses for the people*": I asked what was the present housing set-up. He said he had not an idea, but the *"boys"* would know.'

'*The people*' might have reason to be grateful that he did not know that one of his MPs was a former architect who had specialized in skyscrapers: on his return from the United States, the architect and author, Alfred Charles Bossom, gave up his career as an architect and became Conservative Member for Maidstone in 1931. One day Christopher Soames was sitting with the Prime Minister in the Commons Smoking Room when Churchill asked Soames who '*that fellow over there was*'. 'He was a man of about his own age. I said, "You know him; he's been in the House as long as you have!" "*No*," he said, "*I've never seen him before*." "You have," I said. "He's always been around." "*What's his name?*" I said, "Bossom, Alfred Bossom." "*Good God,*" he said. "*What an extraordinary name – neither one thing nor the other!*"' Bossom was made a baronet in 1953; and life peer in 1960.

During his second premiership Churchill made four official visits to the United States, his first one in January 1952. At one of the conferences to discuss NATO, Field Marshal Slim, then Governor-General of Australia, suggested that the standard issue rifle for NATO forces might be 'a kind of bastard rifle – partly American, partly British'. Churchill asked him to moderate his language: *'It may be recalled that I am myself partly British, partly American.'*

The next time he visited the States, the following year, Truman had been replaced by Dwight D. Eisenhower – General Eisenhower, who had been Supreme Commander of the Allied Expeditionary Force for the invasion of France in 1944, and had for the last three years been Supreme Commander of NATO. Churchill was pleased to have his old friend to deal with, but he and Eisenhower did not always see eye to eye over international affairs. With Stalin's death in 1953, Churchill saw a hope of establishing some sort of friendly relations with Stalin's replacement Malenkov, but Eisenhower was very much against any sort of rapprochement with the Soviets; in any case, Khrushchev soon replaced Malenkov. At Churchill's Bermuda meeting with Eisenhower in December 1953 – while Clementine and their daughter Mary Soames went to Sweden to receive the Nobel Prize for Literature on his behalf – their differing attitudes were all too clear. The hydrogen bomb had been tested a year before and Churchill was quick to grasp the difference between the two nuclear weapons – the hydrogen bomb had terrifying implications not just for world peace but for the survival of the planet. 'Whereas Winston looked on the atomic weapon as something entirely new and terrible,' Jock Colville noted in his diary, Eisenhower 'looked upon it as just the latest improvement in military weapons . . . all weapons in due course became conventional weapons.'

A few months before, Churchill had suffered a serious stroke – yet he was not ready to leave office; he still wanted to save the world, at least from Communist expansion. *'If I stay on for the time being, bearing the burden at my age, it is not because of love for power or office . . .'* he declared. *'If I stay it is because I have a feeling that I may, through things that have happened, have an influence about what I care about above all else – the building of a sure and lasting peace.'*

In June 1954, following another H-bomb test, he went to see Eisenhower again. This time, to Churchill's joy, the President agreed to talks with the Soviets. Everything looked rosy. A tentatively encouraging reply came from Russia. Perhaps Churchill *was* going to save the world, for he had come to believe that the only hope for world peace – and survival – lay ultimately in an agreement with the Russians. But another Soviet message, with unacceptable demands – such as the withdrawal of NATO troops from Europe – and his hopes were cast down. It was time to resign.

'I must retire soon, Anthony [Eden] *won't live for ever.'* These overheard words were uttered only half-jokingly. He was eighty and it was clear that he was not going to preside over a coming-together of the Soviet Union and the United States and Britain. On 1 March 1955, he gave his swansong speech (it was not his last speech, however). Talks on disarmament were not getting anywhere, he pointed out. That left only deterrence to ensure safety and survival over terror and annihilation. *'The day may dawn when fair play, love for one's fellow men, respect for justice and freedom, will enable tormented generations to march forth, serene and triumphant, from the hideous epoch in which we have to dwell. Meanwhile, never flinch, never weary, never despair.'*

*

The last ten years of Churchill's life were comparatively quiet. He and Clementine were not in the best of health, and he had periods of depression (these were not new – he had suffered from bouts, which he called the '*black dog*', all his life – but his ebullience and sense of humour got him out of them quickly enough). But it was a comfortable life, reading and writing, painting, seeing friends. In winter they went south – to the south of France or Marrakech, for instance. They were introduced to Aristotle Onassis, who subsequently entertained them frequently and at length on his yacht or at his Monte Carlo hotel – for no other reason than that his guest was a great man. As for Churchill, he was only too pleased to enjoy the luxurious lifestyle on offer. There were great sadnesses, however, including the suicide of their daughter Diana in 1963.

In 1958 Aneurin Bevan wrote an appreciation of him for the *Observer*, which was not at the time published; perhaps it was thought too valedictory. It was published in the *Guardian* after Churchill's death.

> As a war leader in a democratic country he was without doubt among the greatest. The war was his great chance. He took it. He was cast in the role of the advocate who defended the cause of Great Britain before the world and the destiny of their country before the British people. His name will remain great as long as the war is remembered, as a symbol of what can be done by inspired words when a free and brave people is ready to support them by its actions.

Bevan died in 1960. On hearing of his death, Churchill, in the House of Commons with a group of colleagues at the time, immediately embarked on a eulogy, seeking out and praising his old enemy's good points. Suddenly he stopped, looked round and asked the gathered company: *'Are you sure he's dead?'*

Churchill by now was becoming increasingly dependent upon full-time nurses, and considerably more quiet and withdrawn. In spite of his declining health and strength, however, he still occasionally attended the House of Commons.

On one of his visits to the House of Commons, legend has it, he was sitting alone in an armchair in the Members' bar. Three young Tory MPs came in without seeing him slumped in his chair. 'Sad, isn't it?' remarked one. 'About Winston. He's getting awfully forgetful.'

'Yes. Shame, isn't it?' said another. 'He's really very doddery too now, I gather.'

'Not only that,' the third added, 'but I've heard that he's going a bit – you know – *gaga.'*

'Yes.' A fourth voice issued from the depths of the armchair. *'And they say he's getting terribly* deaf *as well.'*

His last visit to the House of Commons was on 28 July 1964, Churchill having at last stood down as Member for Woodford (for which he needed plenty of persuasion).

During the very early hours of 10 January, Churchill suffered another stroke, this time a massive one, and fell into unconsciousness. It is said that the last intelligible words he uttered were *'I'm so bored with it all,'* spoken as his son-in-law Christopher Soames suggested a glass of champagne. From the 15th it was clear that he would not last long and his doctors issued daily bulletins. His personal detective, Ed Murray, recounts that he visited Churchill as usual on the morning of 23 January:

He was lying on the small bed with his eyes closed and his hands crossed on his breast. He made no response when Howells, the male nurse, announced me, so I stepped forward and placed my right hand in his. It was immediately gripped firmly, and the blue tinge on his face began to disappear, to be replaced by a touch of the old pinkish colour.

The nurse saw this and hurried to present a glass of orange juice to the old man's lips and he sipped from it several times. Howells assured me that was the very first nourishment that had passed those lips in four days. We and young Winston, who had witnessed the event from the open door, began to hope, and Winston and I had a scotch in the lounge: 'He'll do it on them yet again, Sergeant Murray, he'll do it on them yet again.'

Lord Mountbatten remembered that Sir Martin Charteris, Private Secretary to the Queen, rang Jock Colville the moment they had heard the news of his stroke to ask how much longer doctors reckoned he had – 'A day or so?' 'Oh, no,' Colville replied, and went on to tell him that Churchill had once, years before, told him that he would, when the time came, die on the same day as his father – 24 January. Which is exactly what he did.

The tributes poured in, from friends and political foes alike. Only Nelson, Wellington and Gladstone before him had had state funerals – normally for members of royalty only. It was an extraordinary event. From its lying-in-state at Westminster Hall, where over 320,000 queued in the bitter cold to pay their respects, the quarter-ton coffin was drawn slowly along to St Paul's

Cathedral, where the Queen and her family were already seated. Every European monarch or head of state was there, and many others from around the world. The honorary pallbearers included Harold Macmillan, General Lord Ismay, Field Marshal Lord Slim, Marshal of the RAF Lord Portal of Hungerford, the Earl of Avon (Anthony Eden), Earl Attlee, Field Marshal Lord Alexander of Tunis and Admiral of the Fleet Lord Mountbatten of Burma.

After the service the coffin was taken to Tower Steps where it was transferred on to a Port of London Authority launch, the *Havengore*, which took it to Waterloo Station, where it was put on a train which took it to the nearest station to the churchyard at Bladon, in Oxfordshire, hard by Blenheim Palace, where he was buried.

The funeral was seen by millions of television viewers throughout Europe, and many hundreds of millions more across the world listened to it on the radio.

Churchill, who had always needed to be loved, would have been happy to know how much he was in the hearts of millions of people, and would have been gratified by the splendour of the occasion – and pleased that there were nine bands, for the only request he had made regarding his funeral was that there should be lots of bands.

Yet, there were two things he had hoped to achieve and did not. Walter Graebner of *Life* magazine was dining with him in the south of France after having spent a happy afternoon in his company. After a long silence, he suddenly remarked to the assembled guests, *'I have had a wonderful life, full of many achievements. Every ambition I've ever had has been fulfilled – save one.'* What is that? he was asked. *'I am not a great painter,'* he answered.

The other – and there's nothing like setting your sights high – was world peace. More than once he said to Anthony Montague Browne during his last years, *'I worked very hard all my life, and I have achieved a great deal – in the end to achieve nothing.'*

Anybody else would have been happy to have achieved half of what Winston Churchill achieved, which, as he said, was a great deal. But his dream of being the heroic figure directing international affairs towards world peace, as he had once disentangled a traffic jam in Antwerp, was, he knew, never to be fulfilled. Having done much to put it on that course was not enough – he would only be satisfied with the best.

Chronology

Churchill and the Second World War

1939

I September The German Army invades Poland
3 September Britain and France declare war on Germany; WSC
joins Chamberlain's War Cabinet as First Lord of the Admiralty
30 November Russia attacks Finland

1940

8 April The Royal Navy lays mines off Norway's coast; the German
Army invades Denmark and Norway
7–8 May The Norway debate brings Chamberlain's government
down
10 May Germany invades Netherlands, Belgium, Luxembourg;
WSC becomes Prime Minister and Minister of Defence
13 May WSC's first speech as PM: 'blood, toil, tears and sweat'
15 May WSC obtains loan of fifty US destroyers
19 May WSC's broadcast to nation warning of battle to come
27 May Evacuation from Dunkirk begins
4 June WSC's 'never surrender' speech
11 June Italy, under Mussolini, enters war
14 June The German Army enters Paris
18 June WSC warns of possibility of invasion
22 June France signs armistice with Nazi Germany and is divided
into two zones
28 June WSC recognizes Charles de Gaulle as leader of the Free
French

4 July WSC has to order destruction of French fleet in Oran

10 July Battle of Britain starts

20 August WSC gives RAF tribute speech

7 September Start of the Blitz

13 September Italian Army make a rapid advance into Egypt

17 September WSC makes statement on German invasion preparations; calls for establishment of Commando units

27 September Yosuke Matsuoka of Japan signs the Tripartite Pact with Nazi Germany and Italy

9 October WSC becomes leader of Conservative Party

28 October The Italian Army invades Greece

11 November The Fleet Air Arm attacks the Italian Navy at Taranto

14 November The Luftwaffe bombs Coventry

16 November The RAF bombs Hamburg in Germany

19 November The Luftwaffe bombs Birmingham

1941

22 January The British Army captures Tobruk

1 March Bulgaria signs the Tripartite Pact and joins forces with Germany, Italy and Japan

7 March British troops sent to Greece in vain attempt to stop German advance

11 March US Congress passes the Lend-Lease Act

24 March General Erwin Rommel mounts his first attack in the Desert War

6 April The Italian Army in Ethiopia surrenders to Allied forces

10 April Germany, Italy and Bulgaria invade Yugoslavia

14 April Yosuke Matsuoka of Japan signs non-aggression pact with Soviet Union

17 April Yugoslavia surrenders to the German Army

21 April Greece surrenders to the German Army

22 April Evacuation of British troops sent to aid Greece from Greek mainland begins

25 April General Erwin Rommel and his army enter Egypt

10 May The Luftwaffe damages the House of Commons in Westminster; Rudolf Hess flies to Scotland and is arrested by the authorities

24 May The *Bismarck* sinks the British battlecruiser HMS *Hood*

27 May The Royal Navy attacks and sinks the *Bismarck*; British troops evacuated from Crete

15–17 June Wavell replaced as C-in-C North Africa by Auchinleck

22 June Germany invades Russia ('Operation Barbarossa')

12 July Soviet Union and Britain sign agreement of mutual aid; the German Army advances on Leningrad

9–12 August WSC and Roosevelt have shipboard meeting in Placentia Bay, Newfoundland; they sign the Atlantic Charter

6 October The German Army advances on Moscow

7 December Japanese forces attack the US Fleet at Pearl Harbor

8 December Japanese troops invade Malaya, Thailand, Bataan Island in the Philippines

10 December Japanese forces sink the battleships HMS *Prince of Wales* and HMS *Repulse* off the east coast of Malaya

11 December Japanese troops invade Burma

12–30 December WSC at meetings in Washington, DC and Ottawa

18 December Japanese forces invade Hong Kong

25 December Hong Kong surrenders with the loss of its 12,000 garrison

1942

1 January WSC signs United Nations Pact in Washington, DC

11 January Japanese Army captures Kuala Lumpur, the Malayan capital

8 February Japanese troops land on the north-west corner of Singapore

15 February General Arthur Percival surrenders Singapore to Japanese

22 February General Douglas MacArthur and the US forces leave the Philippines

27 March Allied raid on Saint-Nazaire (German submarine base, western France)

30 May Air Marshal Arthur Harris orders the bombing of Cologne

4 June Start of the Battle of Midway, decisive battle between US and Japanese fleets, Midway Islands; victory for US

14 June Rommel defeats General Neil Richie at Gazala

21 June Rommel captures Tobruk

7 August Allied landings at Guadalcanal, Solomon Islands

13 August General Bernard Montgomery is appointed Commander of the British Eighth Army; Alexander appointed C-in-C Middle East

19 August 5,000 Canadian and 1,000 British troops raid the port of Dieppe in France; repulsed with heavy losses

24 August The German Army enters Stalingrad

30 August Rommel attacks Eighth Army at Alam el Halfa

23 October Montgomery orders counter-attack at El Alamein

4 November The German Army defeated at El Alamein

8 November General Dwight D. Eisenhower leads successful Allied invasion of North Africa

13 November The British Army recaptures Tobruk

1943

15–24 January WSC and Roosevelt at Casablanca Conference

18 January The Luftwaffe renews its air attacks on London

23 January The Allies capture Tripoli, Libya

11 May Axis forces surrender in Tunisia

12–13 May German forces in North Africa surrender

16 May Wing Commander Guy Gibson leads the Dam Busters Raid

10 July Allied troops land in German-occupied Sicily

16 July Allies drop leaflets then bombs on mainland Italy

24 July Harris orders further bombing of Hamburg

23 September Italy's new Prime Minister, Pietro Badoglio, signs armistice with the Allies

13 October Badoglio declares war on Germany

18 November RAF begins intensive bombing of Berlin

22 November Start of Tehran Conference between WSC, Roosevelt and Stalin

1944

15 February Allied forces bomb monastery at Monte Cassino

19 February The Luftwaffe makes its heaviest raids on London since May 1941

5 March Orde Wingate launches 'Operation Thursday' in Burma

30 March Allied bombing of Nuremberg

6 June D-Day: the Allies land in Normandy

13 June First V1 flying bomb lands on London

25 August Liberation of Paris

8 September First V2 rocket lands on London

11 September Allied troops enter Nazi Germany

11–16 September WSC and Roosevelt meet in Quebec to discuss post-war Germany

2 October The German Army crushes Warsaw Uprising

4 October The British Army lands in German-occupied Greece

9–17 October WSC, Stalin and Roosevelt meet in Moscow

20 October US Sixth Army lands on Leyte, Philippines

24–28 December WSC visits Athens where discussions lead to truce between local warring factions in January 1945

1945

17 January The Red Army liberates Warsaw

4 February WSC, Stalin and Roosevelt meet at the Yalta Conference

13 February Harris orders the bombing of Dresden

16–17 February WSC meets Middle Eastern heads of state at Cairo and Fayoum

19 February US troops land on Iwo Jima

9 March US Army Air Force creates firestorm in Tokyo

23–26 March Allied armies cross the Rhine

1 April US Army lands on Okinawa

6 April A 700-plane kamikaze attack sinks or damages thirteen US destroyers

7 April The Japanese giant battleship *Yamato* sunk off Okinawa

12 April Roosevelt dies and is replaced by Harry S. Truman

13 April Liberation of Belsen and Buchenwald concentration camps

25 April Liberation of Dachau concentration camp

28 April Benito Mussolini is executed in Milan by Italian partisans

29 April German forces in Italy surrender to the Allies

30 April Adolf Hitler commits suicide

1 May Joseph Goebbels commits suicide

2 May Commander of German troops in Berlin surrenders

4 May All military forces in Germany surrender to the Allies

5 May Denmark liberated by Allied troops

7 May End of the Battle of the Atlantic

8 May VE-Day

5 July General election in Britain

16 July Manhattan Project scientists successfully test atom bomb at Alamogordo, New Mexico

26 July Election results announced. Labour Party under Clement Attlee wins, WSC now leader of the Opposition

6 August US Army Air Force drops atom bomb on Hiroshima

9 August US Army Air Force drops atom bomb on Nagasaki

14 August Japan surrenders unconditionally

2 September VJ Day: General Tomoyuki Yamashita surrenders army in the Philippines; General Douglas MacArthur accepts formal Japanese surrender in Tokyo Bay

6 September Japanese surrender Singapore to Mountbatten

Select Bibliography

CHURCHILL, WINSTON S., *The Story of the Malakand Field Force* (1898); *The World Crisis* (Volumes I: *1911–1914*; II: *1915*; III: *1916–1918*; IV: *The Aftermath;* V: *The Eastern Front*) (1923–31); *My Early Life* (1930); *Thoughts and Adventures* (1932); *Great Contemporaries* (1937); *The History of the Second World War* (Volumes I: *The Gathering Storm*; II: *Their Finest Hour*; III: *The Grand Alliance*; IV: *The Hinge of Fate*; V: *Closing the Ring*; VI: *Triumph and Tragedy*) (1948–54); *Painting as a Pastime* (1948)

BEST, GEOFFREY, *Churchill: A Study in Greatness* (Penguin Books, 2002)

BLAKE, ROBERT, and LOUIS, WILLIAM ROGER, *Churchill* (collected essays by various authors) (Oxford University Press, 1993)

CHURCHILL, RANDOLPH, *Winston S. Churchill*, Volumes I and II (Heinemann, 1990)

COLVILLE, JOHN, *The Churchillians* (Weidenfeld & Nicolson, 1981); *Footprints in Time* (Collins, 1975)

FOUNTAIN, NIGEL, *Voices from the Twentieth Century: The Battle of Britain and the Blitz* (Michael O'Mara Books, 2002)

GILBERT, MARTIN, *Churchill: A Life* (Pimlico, 2000); *In Search of Churchill* (HarperCollins, 1995); *Winston S. Churchill*, Volumes III–VIII (Heinemann, 1971–88); Editor: *Companion Volumes* and *The Churchill War Papers*

HALLE, KAY, The *Irrepressible Churchill* (Robson Books, 2000)

HUMES, JAMES C., *The Wit and Wisdom of Winston Churchill* (HarperCollins, 1995)

JENKINS, ROY, *Churchill* (Pan Macmillan, 2002)

JONES, MADELINE, *Churchill* (World Leaders in Context series)

MONTAGUE BROWNE, ANTHONY, *Long Sunset* (Orion, 1996)

SOAMES, MARY (ed.), *Speaking for Themselves: The Personal Letters of Winston and Clementine Churchill* (Black Swan, 1999)

THOMPSON, W. H., *Sixty Minutes with Winston Churchill* (1953)

There are a number of Churchill websites. The most interesting by far is *www.winstonchurchill.org* – a website maintained by the Churchill Centre and International Churchill Societies, which is wide-ranging and lively, and has useful links.

Thanks are due to Mr Barry Reed, CBE, MC, DL; the late Sir Robert Rhodes James; Mr Mark Seaman and Mr Lance Warrington for their help and information; to Helen Cumberbatch, Gabrielle Mander and Toby Buchan at Michael O'Mara Books for their hard work and help; to Judith Palmer for the picture research, and to Martin Bristow for the design and setting.

Index

dear customer,

i am s. mouse of hayes bros. ltd. and im the boss.
when harry hayes and joe hayes go home for the
night, im in charge.

i can sit on joes swivel chair.
i can put my feet up on harrys desk.

LETTERS FROM A MOUSE

HERBIE BRENNAN

Illustrations by

LOUISE VOCE

WALKER BOOKS
AND SUBSIDIARIES

LONDON • BOSTON • SYDNEY

CR

*To The Maggott
and all my other cats*

H.B.

First published 1997 by Walker Books Ltd
87 Vauxhall Walk, London SE11 5HJ

2 4 6 8 10 9 7 5 3 1

Text © 1997 Herbie Brennan
Illustrations © 1997 Louise Voce

This book has been typeset in Courier.

Printed in Hong Kong

British Library Cataloguing in Publication Data
A catalogue record for this book
is available from the British Library.

ISBN 0-7445-4132-8

J109 705
£6.99

i can sniff around inside the filing cabinet.
i can do anything i want.

but now im in trouble for answering the phone.

last night a man rang up and said, please send me
- a box of carbon paper
- a ream of typing paper, bond
- a ribbon for an ibm electric
- a brief case big enough to hold half a million
  pounds in unmarked 5 pound notes
- a printer stand
- two typing chairs and
- a palatino golf ball.

we dont do sporting goods, i said.
the golf balls for my ibm electric, he said. all
right, i said. all right what, he said. all right
i can send out your order, i said.
now i feel like a rat.
i cant process this mans order because i forgot
to get his name and address. so ive decided to
mail every one of hayes bros. customers on the
computer joe left plugged in.
thats why youve got a copy of this letter. was it
you who talked to me last night. if so, please
write back c/o hayes bros. ltd. and let me know.
its a big order for joe and harry and i wouldnt
like to lose it.
also im sure you need your stuff. you certainly
sounded very anxious about that brief case.

yours sincerely,

s. mouse
hayes bros. ltd.

dear customer,

this is s. mouse of hayes bros. ltd. and im in
bigger trouble than i thought.
a man called up and said, whos this squeaking and
i said, s. mouse of hayes bros. ltd. and he said,
where do you get off, writing to people all over
the country and telling them my business.
i said, what do you mean and he said, i didn't
want anybody to know about the brief case.
why not, i said.
because i want it for my partner, he said.
as a birthday present, i said, and he said,
something like that.
so you want to keep it secret, i said and he gave
a funny laugh and said, yeah, secret, thats it,
secret.
i said, sorry.
he said, thats ok, just send the stuff out pronto
and dont mail any more letters telling people my
business.
yes, sir, i said. pronto, i said.
only in all the excitement i forgot to get his
name and address again.
thats why im writing a second time. even if it
wasnt you who talked to me last night, maybe it
was somebody you know, like your father or your

brother or your uncle.
id like you to ask around. if you find out who it
was who called, ring me at hayes bros. any night.
preferably soon.

yours sincerely,

s. mouse
hayes bros. ltd.

p.s. if it was you i talked to, please note i am
saying no more about the brief case you want for
your partner. i know how to keep a secret.

hayes bros. ltd. OFFICE SUPPLIES

8 Grafton Street, London W1X 3LA England   Tel: 0171 123 4789   Fax: 031 4933061

Directors: J. Hayes H. Hayes

dear customer,

this is s. mouse of hayes bros. ltd. and the
reason i dont use capital letters is i got short
legs.

last night, this guy rang and said, to whom am i
speaking and i said, to s. mouse of hayes bros.
ltd., thats whom.
he said, how come you dont use capital letters in
your letters, they look terrible.
i said, listen, buddy, its no fun standing on a
shift key trying to reach the other keys when you
have legs as short as mine.
he said, i never thought of that. he wasnt the
man who ordered the brief case though. i still
dont know who that was.

but i thought i better let you know about the
capital letters in case you were wondering too.

yours sincerely,

s. mouse
hayes bros. ltd.

hayes bros. ltd. OFFICE SUPPLIES

8 Grafton Street, London W1X 3LA England   Tel: 0171 123 4789   Fax: 031 4933061

Directors: J. Hayes H. Hayes

dear customer,

last night i found a fat envelope in the hayes
bros. post rack addressed personal to s. mouse of
hayes bros. ltd.
so i gnawed it open and inside was 5 thousand
pounds in used 5 pound notes and a handwritten
letter.

the letter said

This is to keep your mouth shut about
the brief case.
Have you sent it out yet? My partner
is due back from Bristol on Monday
so it is getting urgent.
The other stuff doesn't matter –
I only asked for it so the brief case
wouldn't look suspicious.
Just send it out and don't tell Harry
or Joe Hayes.
Or anybody.

P.S. Just make sure it's big enough to
hold half a million cash. Also, I
expect you to move fast.

The letter was not signed and there was no return
address.
have you asked your father and your brother and
your uncle yet. Maybe you should ask around your
cousins too.
thank you.

yours sincerely,

s. mouse
hayes bros. ltd.

p.s. im rich. im rich.

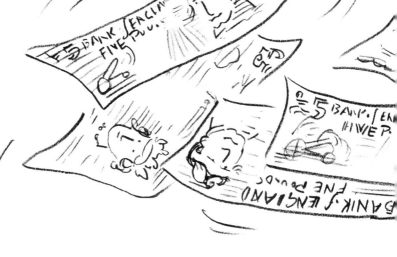

hayes bros. ltd. OFFICE SUPPLIES

8 Grafton Street, London W1X 3LA England   Tel: 0171 123 4789   Fax: 031 4933061

Directors: J. Hayes H. Hayes

DEAR CUSTOMER,

THIS IS S. MOUSE OF HAYES BROS. LTD. AND I HAVE
FOUND THE CAPS LOCK KEY.
THE CAPS LOCK KEY IS RIGHT DOWN ON THE BOTTOM
LEFT OF THIS COMPUTERS KEYBOARD WHICH IS WHY I
DIDNT NOTICE IT BEFORE.
IF YOU JUMP ON THE CAPS LOCK KEY IT STAYS DOWN,
NOT LIKE THE OTHER KEYS WHICH COME UP AGAIN.
WITH THE CAPS LOCK KEY DOWN EVERYTHING PRINTS OUT
IN CAPS.

I STILL CANT DO BRACKETS OR QUOTE MARKS OR THE
QUESTION MARK OR ANYTHING LIKE THAT, BUT I
BELIEVE MY LETTERS WILL LOOK BETTER ALL IN CAPS.
WHAT DO YOU THINK.

NOBODY RANG LAST NIGHT. IT WAS VERY PEACEFUL.

YOURS SINCERELY,

S. MOUSE
HAYES BROS. LTD.

DEAR CUSTOMER,

THIS IS S. MOUSE OF HAYES BROS. LTD. AND MY
FRIEND COCKROACH HAS GOT ME WORRIED.
COCKROACH DROPS IN TO SEE ME SOMETIMES AFTER JOE
AND HARRY GO HOME.
LAST NIGHT SHE SAID, YOU SHOULD BE CAREFUL ABOUT
SENDING OUT ANY BRIEF CASE BIG ENOUGH TO HOLD
HALF A MILLION SOVS.
WHAT ARE SOVS, I SAID.
POUNDS, DONT YOU KNOW ANYTHING.
I DONT KNOW SOVS, I SAID. WHY SHOULD I BE CAREFUL
ABOUT SENDING OUT THE BRIEF CASE.
SHE SAID, BECAUSE IT SOUNDS VERY SUSPICIOUS TO
ME. I SAID WHY. SHE SAID, THERE WAS A ROBBERY IN
BRISTOL ON TUESDAY.
THATS WHERE THIS MANS PARTNER IS COMING BACK
FROM, I SAID. COCKROACH SAID, I KNOW.
I SAID, HOW MUCH WAS TAKEN IN THE ROBBERY IN
BRISTOL AND SHE SAID, HALF A MILLION POUNDS.
I SAID, OH.

NOW IM CONFUSED. COCKROACH SAID I SHOULD PHONE
THE POLICE, BUT I DIDNT BECAUSE HARRY HAS BEEN
GIVING OUT TO JOE ABOUT THE SIZE OF THE PHONE
BILL.
BESIDES, IF I TELL THE POLICE ABOUT THE BRIEF
CASE THEY WOULD JUST LAUGH AT ME BECAUSE I DONT
KNOW THE MANS NAME AND ADDRESS.
THEY MIGHT ALSO WANT TO KNOW ABOUT THE 5 THOUSAND
POUNDS IN USED 5 POUND NOTES.
DO YOU THINK THE MAN WHO WANTS THE BRIEF CASE HAS
ANYTHING TO DO WITH THE ROBBERY IN BRISTOL.
AND WHAT SHOULD I DO IF HE PHONES AGAIN.
I WOULD VERY MUCH LIKE TO HAVE YOUR OPINION ON
THESE MATTERS.

YOURS SINCERELY,

S. MOUSE
HAYES BROS. LTD.

P.S. COCKROACH ISNT REALLY A COCKROACH, THATS
JUST HER NICKNAME. SHES A SPIDER.

dear customer,

this is s. mouse of hayes bros. ltd. and i have
broken the caps lock key.
i jumped up and down on it too hard and it broke.

cockroach says they dont make them like they used
to, but i think it broke because i got too
excited.
the man rang again last night and said, listen,
are you trying to mouse me up. you mean louse
you up, i said and he said, no, i mean mouse me
up. no, sir, i said, im not trying to mouse
anybody up.
he said, i suppose youll try to tell me you didnt
get the money i sent.
no, sir, i said, i wouldnt try to tell you that
at all.

then wheres my brief case, he said.
so i told him there was a problem. we are right
out of stock of brief cases, i said, but he didnt
believe me.
he said if he didnt get his brief case before
thursday he would put out a contract on me with a
hit cat.
then he hung up.
i still didnt get his name and address.
its been one of those nights.
cockroach said i should send him back the 5
thousand pounds. how can i, i said, when i dont
know his name and address. you are a plonker, i
said.
cockroach looked squashed.
if you hear anything at all about the robbery in
bristol, please phone me.

yours sincerely,

s. mouse
hayes bros. ltd.

p.s. actually, we arent out of stock on brief
cases at all. i only told him that. if you were
going to buy a brief case from hayes bros. ltd.,
i wouldnt want to mislead you.

p.p.s. maybe cockroach is right about the police.
getting laughed at is better than getting eaten
by a hit cat. ill sleep on it and maybe ring them
up tomorrow night.

dear customer,

this is s. mouse of hayes bros. ltd. and i would
appreciate it if you would consider doing me a
favour.
last night a woman phoned and said, is that
s. mouse and i said, yes, maam, this is s. mouse
of hayes bros. ltd. and she said, are you for real.
im for hayes bros. ltd., i said.
no, she said, i mean are you a real live mouse or
are you just some sort of publicity stunt.
then, before i could answer her, she said, i
mean, i keep getting these crazy letters from a
mouse and at first i thought they were just
written by some bozo trying to sell me office
supplies but now im not so sure so i decided to
phone up and find out for myself and here i am
actually talking to a mouse, for heavens sake.
and you certainly do talk a lot, i thought, but i
didnt say that. what i said was, maam, i am a
real mouse, i am not some bozo trying to sell you
office supplies.

then how come you can talk and type and do stuff
that other mice cant, she said.

i took a course in business administration, i
said.

then after that a man rang up and said, is that
s. mouse of hayes bros. ltd. yuk, yuk, yuk.

i said, this is he.

the man said, how would you like to come and work
for me, mouse, or may i call you s. yuk, yuk,
yuk.

no thank you, sir, i said. i am very happy
working here at hayes bros. ltd.

you could make a lot of money working for me,
yuk, yuk, yuk, he said.

i already have an elegant sufficiency, i said,
thinking about the 5 thousand pounds in the fat
envelope.

you slay me, mouse, you really do, the man said.

i wish i could, i said, but he didnt hear me.

these calls took up so much of my time i didnt
get to ring the police.
as a favour, could you not call me up to ask if
im for real or go yuk, yuk, yuk down the phone.
but do ring if you hear anything about the
robbery in bristol or the guy who wants the brief
case.

or if you want to buy any office supplies, of
course.

yours sincerely,

s. mouse
hayes bros. ltd.

hayes bros. ltd. OFFICE SUPPLIES

8 Grafton Street, London W1X 3LA England   Tel: 0171 123 4789   Fax: 031 4933061

Directors: J. Hayes H. Hayes

dear customer,

this is s. mouse of hayes bros. ltd. and my
friend cockroach told me british telecom dont
charge if you make a 999 call.
that finally persuaded me to ring the police.

old bill here, the policeman said.

hello, bill, i said, this is s. mouse of hayes
bros. ltd., and i want to report a robbery of,
half a million pounds.

was that the one in bristol, he said.

yes, sir, i said. i have this man who wants me to
send him out a brief case and i think he plans to
use it to smuggle out the money.

do you have this mans name and address, bill
asked me.

no, sir, i admitted, i forgot to get it. i waited
for him to laugh at me, but he didnt.

is he likely to phone you again, he asked.
its possible, i said.

maybe we could put a tap on your phone, he said.
do you think harry hayes and joe hayes would
agree.

they might, i said, they use a lot of water to
make coffee.

actually i didnt think harry and joe would agree
to messing up their phone at all, but i didn't
want to argue since old bill was so nice.

one good thing though, he promised to send a
squad car round each night to keep an eye out for
the hit cat.

i am writing so you will realize our police are
wonderful.

yours sincerely,

s. mouse
hayes bros. ltd.

hayes bros. ltd. OFFICE SUPPLIES

8 Grafton Street, London W1X 3LA England   Tel: 0171 123 4789   Fax: 031 4933061

Directors: J. Hayes H. Hayes

dear customer,

this is s. mouse of hayes bros. ltd. and that
noise inside joe hayes office is the cat.

he got in through the skylight while the
policemen in the patrol car were on their tea
break.

i should have known he might try something like
that since he was a professional.
fortunately joe hayes always locks his office
door when he goes home for the night, so the hit
cat cant get at me.

i was expecting him, of course, this being well
past thursday and i still havent been able to
send out the brief case.
when i heard him coming in, i made sure joes door
was locked. then i stuck my head through the
mousehole in the skirting and hurled abuse at
him.

he didnt like that.

when he found he couldnt get at me, he tried to
go back out onto the roof, but my friend
cockroach had closed the skylight.
so now hes trapped. and hes going to be in big
trouble when joe hayes comes in tomorrow because
i know for a fact joe is allergic to cats.

i guess that puts paid to one threat to my life.
i knew you would want to know.

yours sincerely,

s. mouse
hayes bros. ltd.

dear customer,

this is s. mouse of hayes bros. ltd. and im still
shaking like a leaf.

last night the man called about the brief case,
but not on the phone.
he rang the doorbell sometime after midnight and
when i wouldnt open up, he let himself in with a
credit card.
where are you, s. mouse, he shouted. i am going to
stomp you for what you done to my hit cat.
that wasnt me, i thought, that was joe hayes, but
i didnt want to argue since he was so big.
where are you, he called out again, where are you,
where are you.
i was inside the computer examining the circuitry,
but i didnt tell him. he opened up the filing
cabinet and all the desk drawers and he turned out
the waste-basket, all the time shouting, where are
you, s. mouse, where are you.

he looked behind the radiator and pulled some
books down off the shelves. he even looked inside
harry hayes liquor cabinet even though i am
teetotal.

then he quietened down a little and got this
funny look on his face and came over to the
computer.

i thought he was on to me but he just sat down
and switched on the computer and typed a
message.

i have merged his message with this letter so
you can read what he wrote.

*You can't hide for ever, S. Mouse. You
think you are smart just because you
took my five grand and didn't send the
case. Well, let me tell you, nobody puts
one over on me. I have trapped better
mice than you. I'll be back after my
partner and I stash the money and when I
do, you'd better look out. You'll wish
you had never been born, S. Mouse. What
does the "S" in your name stand for
anyway? I bet it stands for SCUMBAG!*

it was an abusive letter, but very well typed.
when he was done, he put down a piece of cheese,
stole a brief case and left.

i am writing so you will know what i am up
against.

also, will you keep your eyes open for a big
abusive man carrying a brief case that looks as
if it might contain half a million pounds.
if you see him, dont wait to ring me, call the
police and ask for my friend old bill.
tell him s. mouse of hayes bros. ltd. said you
were to call.

im sure he will remember me.

yours sincerely,

s. mouse
hayes bros. ltd.

p.s. my fur is no longer standing up on end and
the ringing in my ears has stopped. all the same,
it is no fun being inside a computer when
somebody switches on and writes a letter.
p.p.s. i ignored the cheese. im not stupid.

dear customer,

this is s. mouse of hayes bros. ltd.
last night my friend cockroach called from
heathrow airport and told me the crooks were on
a plane to south america.
i said, are you all right, cockroach, and she
said, sure, it was a bit hot inside that brief
case but otherwise im fine.
i said, stick around and watch the fun. then
i called old bill.

i said, this is s. mouse of hayes bros. ltd. and
the guys who did the bristol robbery are just
about to board a plane for south america.

how do you know, he said.

i had them bugged, i said.

well get some squad cars round, he said.
just make sure theyre not on their tea break,
i said.
but old bill didnt hang about. his men snatched
the robbers right out on the tarmac.

all the money was in a hayes bros. brief case one
of them was carrying, except for 5 thousand
pounds which the police said had mysteriously

disappeared. cockroach got a lift back in the squad car.

you may have read about it in the papers. mouse makes mincemeat of robbers escape plan.

yours sincerely,

s. mouse
hayes bros. ltd.

MOUSE MAKES MINCEMEAT OF ROBBERS ESCAPE PLAN

The massive £500,000 bank robbery in Bristol has now been solved ... by a mouse.

Timely action by S. Mouse of Hayes Bros. Ltd., a London office supply company, and his arachnid partner Cockroach, led to the apprehension of the robbers only minutes before they were set to make their escape to South America.

Mr Mouse told our reporters he became suspicious when one of the robbers ordered a brief case from Hayes Bros. Ltd. of the exact size needed to hold the money stolen in the robbery.

On Mouse's instructions, his colleague Cockroach hid in the brief case and alerted Mouse by phone from Heathrow

airport when she discovered the robbers were about to leave the country. Mouse then called the police.

Plain-clothes detectives and uniformed patrolmen rushed to the airport and managed to apprehend the criminals as they were boarding the plane.

"They were armed and dangerous," said Inspector Katchum of the Yard. "If it hadn't been for the tip-off from the mouse, they would almost certainly have gotten clean away."

There is speculation that both S. Mouse and Cockroach are in line for Duke of Edinburgh Awards for bravery and may even be recommended for the New Year's Honours list.

hayes bros. ltd. OFFICE SUPPLIES

8 Grafton Street, London W1X 3LA England   Tel: 0171 123 4789   Fax: 031 4933061

Directors: J. Hayes H. Hayes

dear customer

this is s. hayes of mouse bros. ltd. and ive been
celebrating. ive stopped being teetotal this one
time because harry and joe read all about me in
the paper.

they were so pleased about the free publicity for
hayes bros. ltd. that they gave me a promotion.
also a substantial raise.

im very glad the way things have turned out.

yours sincerely,

s. mouse
night manager
hayes bros. ltd.